Toolkit for College Success

The Wadsworth College Success™ Series

College Study Skills: Becoming a Strategic Learner
   by Diana Van Blerkom (1994)

Integrating College Study Skills: Reasoning in Reading, Listening, and Writing, Third Edition
   by Peter Elias Sotiriou (1993)

Mastering Mathematics: How to Be a Great Math Student, Second Edition
   by Richard Manning Smith (1994)

Merlin: The Sorcerer's Guide to Survival in College
   by Christopher F. Monte (1990)

The Mountain is High Unless You Take the Elevator: Success Strategies for Adult Learners
   by Laurence N. Smith and Timothy L. Walter (1992)

Right from the Start: Managing Your Way to College Success
   by Robert Holkeboer (1993)

Toolkit for College Success
   by Daniel R. Walther (1994)

Turning Point
   by Joyce D. Weinsheimer (1993)

The Freshman Year Experience™ Series

College is Only the Beginning: A Student Guide to Higher Education, Second Edition
   by John N. Gardner and A. Jerome Jewler (1989)

Create Your College Success: Activities and Exercises for Students
   by Robert A. Friday (1988)

The Power to Learn: Helping Yourself to College Success
   by William E. Campbell (1993)

Step by Step to College Success
   by John N. Gardner and A. Jerome Jewler (1987)

Your College Experience: Strategies for Success
   by John N. Gardner and A. Jerome Jewler (1992)

Your College Experience: Strategies for Success, Concise Edition
   by A. Jerome Jewler and John N. Gardner,
   with Mary-Jane McCarthy (1993)

The Senior Year Experience™ Series

Ready for the Real World
   by Bill Hartel, Stephen Schwartz, Steven Blume,
   and John N. Gardner (1994)

Toolkit for College Success

Daniel R. Walther

Brazosport College

Wadsworth Publishing Company

Belmont, California
A DIVISION OF WADSWORTH, INC.

The Wadsworth College Success Series™ Editor: Angela Gantner

Editorial Assistant: Lisa Timbrell

Developmental Editor: John Boykin

Production Editor: Wendy Earl

Text Designer: Design Office Bruce Kortebein, San Francisco

Cover Designer: Stephen Rapley

Cover Painting: Robert Hunt

Print Buyer: Randy Hurst

Permissions Editor: Robert Kauser

Copy Editor: Sally Peyrefitte

Illustrator, tools: Chris Spollen, Moonlight Press

Illustrator, icons: John R. Nelson

Compositor: Design Office, San Francisco

Printer: Courier, Kendallville, Indiana

This book is printed on acid-free recycled paper.

I(T)P™

International Thomson Publishing
The trademark ITP is used under license

Printed in the United States of America

1 2 3 4 5 6 7 8 9 10 — 98 97 96 95 94

Library of Congress Cataloging-in-Publication Data

Walther, Daniel R., 1949–
   Toolkit for college success / Daniel R. Walther.
     p. cm.
   Includes index.
   ISBN 0-534-23052-0 (acid-free paper)
   1. College student orientation. 2. Study skills I. Title.
LB2343.3.W35   1994   93-41927
378.1'7028'12—dc20   CIP

To my father—a craftsman of tools;
To Phyllis, Casey, and Zack—for their love and support;
and
To four educators—
Ms. Maude Kreig, Ms. Zora Smith, Dr. Norman Peterson
and Dr. Thomas Brasher—
for their inspired teaching and encouragement

Contents

11 Getting Results from Research

Becoming a Skilled Researcher

Preface to the Instructor

From the time the notion of writing a textbook popped into my head and on through the latter stages of the book's production, a persistent metaphor kept asserting itself: Students need a *toolkit* to equip them for the challenging work ahead of them in college. This toolkit should include tools used for thinking and tools applicable to specific learning tasks. It should be concise, adaptable, and user-friendly. I hope that as you examine this text, you will find it a successful rendering of that metaphor.

The following thematic notions that underlie the basic nature of the book give the students a new perspective on the learning process that can motivate them to excellence.

1. Learning theory can be made palatable to students, and it is essential to producing long-term behavioral changes.

When I began teaching study skills on a college campus in 1988, I was taken aback by a student's question that I have heard many times since: "Why didn't anybody teach us this years ago?" I had to confront what was obvious to many of my students: while spending thousands of hours trying to teach the specifics of the academic disciplines to each student, we have left unexamined important principles of learning that could have made the students' tasks more manageable. It is almost as if we assumed that students were like birds that would naturally learn to fly if we just nudged them out of the nest. For most students, the skills required by the formal education process are *not* instinctive and natural. Students need flight school, and the early lessons should be aimed at the principles of flight, not just the instruments in the cockpit.

This book takes the viewpoint that learning theory is relevant to every college student. Most students have an untapped reservoir of curiosity about how learning "happens." *Toolkit for College Success* attempts to tap into that sense of curiosity and motivate students to apply these new ideas in powerful and exciting ways.

My premise is that study skills texts must ground the strategies they teach in sound learning theory to ensure student success. Failure to do so only feeds the phenomenon all too often lamented by teachers of study skills: "We can teach the students effective strategies, but we just can't get them to use them." I am convinced that students can be willing and active inquirers into issues like learning styles, the "construction" of knowledge, the process of reading, the nature of our memory, and the structure and objectives of academic discourse. I have made every effort to segue naturally from relevant learning theory to the application of specific tools, tips, and templates that use the theory.

2. At the heart of learning is a very basic process that only the student can initiate: the process of confronting and interacting with information to construct usable knowledge.

There are many external factors that can influence the learning process: the atmosphere of the institution and the classroom, the skill of the textbook writer, the teaching style of the instructor, and so on. But the best imaginable combination of such factors is no more than an efficient information delivery system. Education comes down to the one-on-one confrontation that occurs between the student and the material, and students who avoid that confrontation will not learn effectively. Students take a giant step toward academic success when they accept responsibility for creating personal knowledge out of the information presented. This notion of student accountability in the process of learning is introduced early in the book and is reinforced throughout.

To assist students in their effort to construct usable knowledge, *Toolkit for College Success* provides graphic aids that serve as navigational elements throughout the text. These elements help relate the parts of the chapter to its overall focus. I hope that these elements make the text both user-friendly and highly motivational.

3. Students can profit as learners by observing the collegiate educational system through their teachers' eyes.

Toolkit for College Success helps students understand the teacher's role in the educational process. Students are encouraged to view the campus as a community with certain values or codes of conduct applied to academic pursuits. Faculty members—themselves successful products of that community—are a very homogenous group with fairly predictable expectations about what students must do to become members of that learning community. *Toolkit for College Success* helps students anticipate faculty members' expectations about testing, including what tests represent and how tests are constructed and graded. The text also gives extensive treatment to the issue of "academic communication"— elements of structure, language, documentation, and ethics.

4. Students can make dramatic improvement in their work by developing their metacognitive abilities.

Toolkit for College Success encourages students to occasionally step out of the roles they play as readers, note takers, writers, reviewers, and constructors of knowledge, and play the roles of observers and critics. At various points in the text, they are encouraged to pose questions like, "How well am I understanding this?" "What mental task was I doing just now?" "Why is this so difficult for me to learn?" "Why is this test score better than my last one?" Students who join in the dialogue on how learning takes place are poised to learn another valuable skill—the ability of the mind to monitor its own processes.

Pedagogical Issues

Focus   *Toolkit* has a narrower focus than some of the texts offered for freshman seminar programs or study skills classes. I have taught from comprehensive textbooks myself, and I have always felt guilty asking students to buy texts that covered so many topics we would not have time to cover. I wanted to keep this book as concise and adaptable as possible, directing the content at learning theory and study skills rather than issues like money management, health issues, or drug and alcohol abuse. These are certainly important topics, but I believe that the most useful approach is to provide a strong core text in study skills and let instructors supplement it with materials suited to their particular student population. Health and social issues often lend themselves to treatments involving special speakers or a variety of nontextual resources.

Background Theory   Freshman seminars and study skills courses are taught by faculty and staff members from diverse backgrounds; we cannot assume that study skills are the sole province of the reading or English faculty. The learning theory in this text, while addressed to the student, provides important background concepts for instructors whose primary discipline may not have focused on educational theory.

Flexibility   *Toolkit* recognizes that different instructors will have varied opinions on the best sequence of chapters for study, so the book format is flexible, in keeping with the toolkit metaphor. Students and instructors are encouraged to rummage through its contents, picking and choosing ideas and tools they find most relevant or adaptable. I strongly recommend that the first chapter be the initial focus of a class, because some of the thematic issues discussed earlier in this preface are introduced in that chapter. The remaining chapters are relatively self-contained; no single chapter requires an antecedent to the learning theory and skills it teaches.

Application   Some of the most successful activities and exercises are included in the instructor's manual because I believe that the best exercises lose some of their dramatic effect when students have the opportunity to preview them in advance. I consistently get more spontaneous responses and memorable results from exercises that I "spring" on the students.

Features   Perhaps the most obvious pedagogical elements in the book are its showier components: the tips, tools, and templates. These are designed to help students translate the theory into action.

 Tips are narrow, independent strategies that students can apply with little or no background knowledge. They are a collection of proven "nifty ideas" that can be easily put to use.

 Tools provide a detailed, cohesive skills system that is an outgrowth of the learning theory introduced in each chapter. Tools are more complicated than tips and usually require student practice.

 Templates give the students initial "mental structures" while they are learning to use the tools. Students may absorb the learning theory and have a general sense of how the tool is to be used, but most will need the guidance and support that templates provide. Their initial guidance and support help students use an inductive process to develop a richer understanding of the theory and tools. After students learn to apply specific skills through using the templates, encourage them to adapt and fine-tune the templates to meet the needs of a particular class. With a little experimentation, students may become their own intellectual toolmakers.

Acknowledgments

I would like to acknowledge the valuable contributions of those people who helped bring this text to print. First, I would like to thank Wadsworth editor Angie Gantner, whose enthusiastic support and able guidance helped me shape the book into what I had hoped it could be. Thanks also to Lisa Timbrell, editorial assistant, to John Boykin and Sarah Hubbard for their valuable content suggestions, and to Kathy Hartlove for her guidance on the production of the instructor's manual. Let me also acknowledge and thank Wendy Earl for producing the manuscript and Bruce Kortebein for his creative design work.

I appreciate the valuable feedback of five educators who took time out of their schedules to review the manuscript:

Anne Teigen, Tacoma Community College

Michael Radis, Pennsylvania State University

Christine Roth, University of Texas

Barry Stearns, Lansing Community College

Fran Zaniello, Northern Kentucky University

Finally, thanks to my colleagues and friends at Brazosport College for their encouragement and kind wishes.

I welcome your reactions to this text and any suggestions you may have to make it more useful. You may respond to the questionnaire at the end of the text and/or contact me through Wadsworth Publishing Company, 10 Davis Drive, Belmont, CA 94002.

Dan Walther

FIGURE 1.1

THEORY   TIPS   TOOLS   TEMPLATES

The Toolbox Contents

You will encounter four primary study skills approaches in *Toolkit for College Success:* theory, tips, tools, and templates.

Each study skill section is easily identifiable by its logo and its color bar.

Theory

As the symbol suggests, the theory sections are designed to help you get your "mind in gear" before you tackle the more specific tools and templates. Sections marked with this symbol present important background information about learning, information that either justifies the use of the tools or templates or makes their purpose clearer.

Tips

Tips are brief, easy-to-apply strategies that you can use immediately. They don't really require much background understanding. In many cases, they represent simple, proven strategies that you may react to by wondering, "Now why didn't I think of this years ago?"

Tools

The theory section of each chapter helps you develop a different "mind set" toward a particular task, and tools translate that mind set into action. While tips are narrow, individual strategies, a tool is a system made up of linked steps or strategies. Taken together, these represent an entirely different approach to a major learning task.

Templates

Just as a draftsman's templates provide for accurate and well-structured work, the templates in *Toolkit for College Success* are designed to help you do your academic work more efficiently. Most of the templates are specialized forms, which you may want to reproduce with a copy machine and use on a daily or weekly basis. The templates help guide both the way you organize the information you are dealing with and the way you "see" it. As you will learn further on in the pages of *Toolkit*, the way in which information is structured and organized has a major impact on how easily it can be recalled.

What Successful Students Know

What *do* successful students know? On first consideration, you might say that successful students know how to factor equations, work chemistry problems, read (and understand!) Shakespeare, and so on. But what successful students have learned that their less successful counterparts have not is not just a question of subject matter skills. It has to do with underlying knowledge about learning itself. Few students have really been taught this underlying knowledge, since the educational system has not really made an effort to focus directly on these skills. The more successful students have simply learned, through a process of trial and error, that certain behaviors improve their performance. The six skills that are explained below reflect important principles on which the contents of *Toolkit for College Success* are based.

1 Successful students relate their class work to clearly defined long-range goals.

Many educators lament the lack of motivation they see in some of the students who struggle through school. Many students' academic records are marked by a trail of mediocre grades, dropped classes, excessive absence reports, and so on. These students will readily admit that they have a problem with motivating themselves to do their class work. Perhaps they fail to see the relevance of college algebra, art appreciation, history, or other curricular requirements. Their long-range goals are cloudy at best. As one modern-day philosopher has suggested, "Education is one of the few things people are willing to pay for and not get."

Successful students have much more clearly defined goals. They have taken the initiative to meet with a counselor and consider career or life options. They have established a major and have a much clearer picture in mind of where they are headed and how the courses they are taking contribute to that "big picture." Grades, attendance requirements, and assignments take on a new meaning because they represent intermediate steps on the way to reaching the long-range goals. As a result, these students are more highly motivated.

> *The tragedy of life doesn't lie in not reaching your goal. The tragedy lies in having no goal to reach.*
>
> BENJAMIN MAYS

2 Successful students take control of their educational experiences.

The students who succeed do so largely because they see themselves as the central person in their educational experiences. To use a term psychologists favor, such students have an "internal locus of control." They play an active role in guiding and shaping the events

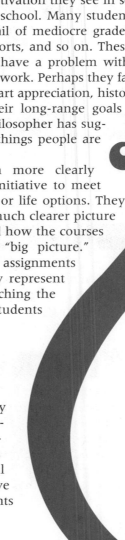

around them to their advantage.

Students who have an "external locus of control" react very differently. They often see themselves as victims in the educational system, almost powerless to affect the circumstances around them. They registered late and got the toughest history teacher in the department. Their economics teacher is a really boring lecturer. The reading list from their English class has nothing that remotely interests them. Their speech teacher has assigned them to work on a group project with the three laziest students in the class. Students who do not see themselves as the ones responsible for their education often look at teachers as the "crucial variable" in getting an education: if they get a "good" teacher, an interesting teacher, a teacher who uses the test format they like, then everything will work out fine. If not, they're doomed. Such students play a passive role; things "happen" to them, and they don't really see themselves in a position to do much about it.

Students who have learned to achieve in the educational system refuse to be passive victims. If they get the toughest teacher in the history department, they budget extra time to work with the subject or perhaps organize a study group of classmates to pool their collective understanding of the material. If they get a boring lecturer, they move to the front of the class as a way to stay more actively involved, or perhaps they use a creative note-taking method such as "concept-mapping" to add interest to the class or make the time go faster. When faced with a reading list that doesn't offer any interesting works, they go to their teacher's office and try to negotiate an acceptable alternative work. When teamed up with unmotivated workers on a project, they take the initiative to lead the group and make sure progress is made. In short, they act in positive ways to exert control over their own education.

Champions take responsibility. When the ball is coming over the net, you can be sure I want the ball.

BILLIE JEAN KING

3 Successful students have learned to be aware of their own learning and thinking processes.

Effective learners have the ability to "eavesdrop" on their own thought processes, to think about their thinking. They are able to observe and monitor their own experiences and emotions and make adjustments in their behaviors that lead to productive results. They have a voice inside their head that sends messages about such behaviors: "My mind is wandering, and I'm not understanding this reading assignment. I need to put it aside and take a break for a few minutes." "Why didn't I get more credit on this essay test item? What did I leave out?" "I don't understand these notes very well…. I'd better go by to see the teacher for some help." "I did a lot better on this algebra test than on the first one…. Working the extra problems in each chapter must really be helping me."

This ability of learners to "pull back" and observe their own efforts at thinking and learning will enable them to exert greater control over the learning process.

An intellectual is a person whose mind watches itself.

ALBERT CAMUS

4 Successful students recognize that understanding takes place over time; it is seldom immediate.

Real understanding seldom comes to people like a lightning bolt. Our working memory absorbs information very quickly, but its "hold" on the information is seldom lasting: much of the detail we store in our working memory will fade away in less than a day. Effective students have learned that understanding new information requires review and reinforcement. They discipline themselves to spend a little time each day and each week to process details in their working memory to construct knowledge and absorb it into their long-term memory. Since they recognize the futility of trying to learn huge amounts of information in an all-night cram session the night before a major exam, their test preparation is much less frantic. They process information as it comes in and work at *overlearning* difficult information to decrease the "brain drain" that would otherwise occur over time.

5 Successful students use more than one sensory channel to improve their learning.

Learning theorists today believe that people learn by different processes and through different "channels." Many researchers believe that the left hemisphere of the brain, the center for speech and language, functions most effectively handling details sequentially and performing logical or analytical processes. The right hemisphere is thought to be the center for our emotional behavior, to absorb information more "holistically," and to function most effectively with visual and spatial details. Although some psychologists balk at labeling people as either right- or left-brained learners, there is a consensus on the notion that learning takes place most effectively when information is processed in a way that involves both left and right brain processes.

Many successful students have learned to take information best suited to left brain processes—the verbal world of textbooks and class lectures—and transform it into visual images, concept maps that represent information in charts or diagrams with clear spatial relationships, or some other physical or tactile form.

6 Successful students look for underlying structure in what they are learning.

High-achieving students attempt to determine the deeper structure that underlies the information they are trying to learn. When listening to a teacher's lecture or discussion, they try to imagine the outline or plan the teacher is working from. They preview a reading assignment before they begin to read in order to see the skeleton of main points that give the chapter its structure. When reviewing details in their class notes, they mentally arrange these details into forms or groups that will make it easier to recall them on a test. When preparing writing assignments or oral presentations, these students clearly structure the information so that the reader or listener will not have to struggle to see how the main ideas are related.

Students who have mastered the process of learning are not always the most brilliant people on campus. They have, however, adopted most of the characteristics cited above. While the theories behind these characteristics have only briefly been introduced above, as you begin to sample the contents of your *Toolkit for College Success*, you will start to develop these same characteristics and become better educated on the process of learning.

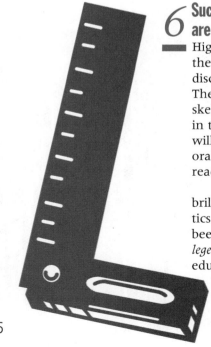

Each mind has its own method.

RALPH WALDO EMERSON

We know what we are, but know not what we may be. SHAKESPEARE'S HAMLET

On the Capacity to Change

Shakespeare had us pegged pretty well. Each of us has a definite sense of who and what we are, but seldom do we dare to dream of what we can become. So it is appropriate to take some time to address what may be the most important notion in this book: that *you are capable of reshaping yourself as a student and as a person.*

Chances are pretty good that you have a distinct impression of yourself as a student, both your strengths and your weaknesses. Perhaps you see yourself as a good English student but a poor math student, good at classroom discussions but a poor test taker, a klutz in physical education courses but a whiz in front of a computer. How did you get those impressions? Were you born with those capabilities and judgments, or did they develop over a period of years? Although it may be true that we are born with certain mental capacities, we also know that our assessment of ourselves is shaped significantly by the people around us and by our experiences. Let's consider how a powerful phenomenon called a *self-fulfilling prophecy* can shape students' perceptions of themselves.

Self-Fulfilling Prophecy

Psychologists tell us that we do not develop a self-concept in a vacuum. We depend a great deal on direct experiences with others to help us mold a self-concept. Much of that self-concept is developed through a process called reflected appraisal. We get a "glimpse" of ourselves based on the feedback we receive from others. Each of us is like a mirror, and the nature of the feedback sent, either positive or negative, contributes to the overall opinions we have of ourselves. In extreme cases bordering on emotional abuse, children who are repeatedly given back harshly negative "reflections" grow up seeing themselves as unworthy and incompetent. At the opposite extreme are children trying to be molded by unrealistic, unrelenting positive reflections into something a parent wants them to be, perhaps the most popular boy or girl in the school, the musical prodigy, or the super athlete. Luckily, for the majority of children, the feedback is less extreme and more balanced, but sometimes events conspire to produce a "deficiency" that could have been avoided. Let's imagine a simple scenario.

Jennifer, who is in the seventh grade, is an average to above-average math student. One night, as she prepares for a math test, going over some returned homework on some prealgebra concepts, her mother walks into the room. Mom notices what Jennifer is working on and makes an innocent, off-the-cuff comment: "I hope you got your dad's brains when it comes to math. I remember how algebra used to give me fits. I was lucky to make it out of that class with a C." Unintentionally, Jennifer's mother may have just planted a seed. If Jennifer takes this comment to mean that math skills are somehow hereditary or that males have an inborn math aptitude that females don't, the remark may alter both her attitude and her behavior. Her mother's comment may cause Jennifer to study differently, perhaps simply to be less focused on her math review and more focused on her mother's comments. Perhaps she is a little more anxious and intimidated the next day when she goes in to take her math quiz, can't concentrate as well as in the past, or perhaps second-guesses herself and changes a few answers. The result: her test score is a letter grade or two lower than her previous grades, perhaps a 65 rather than an 80 or so.

Now Jennifer has both her mother's comment and the feedback of a poorer grade to consider. The two combined may make her just that much more anxious two weeks later, when she takes her next math test. As a result, she gets another low grade and perhaps an expression of concern from her math teacher. It is not difficult to imagine this scenario repeating itself, until at some time in the future Jennifer can be heard muttering to herself, "I just have a really tough time with algebra." Because the pattern has been repeated often enough, Jennifer sees herself as—and has in fact become—a poor math student. She takes less challenging math courses and arrives some years later as a college freshman with a clear sense of limitations in her head about the career choices open to her, because she's a "poor math student."

A self-fulfilling prophecy doesn't always have to be negative. After her mother's innocent observation, Jennifer may respond differently. Perhaps she feels a special kinship to her father, the "good math student," and assumes that she may have a natural math aptitude. She might show a little spunk and

decide to prove to her parents that she can be a good math student if she really wants to. Her expectations and behavior move her in another direction: she studies that much harder, goes into the test with greater confidence, aces it, graciously accepts her teacher's praise, and vows to continue working hard to get more positive "reflections" in the future. She has started off on a much more positive tack and arrives as a college freshman with her sights set on a degree in engineering.

Those scenarios, although they are perhaps a bit too simplistic, nevertheless depict what has happened to each of us to some degree. The self-fulfilling prophecy begins as a cycle: an expectation, or fear, is created, which produces a change in behavior or in our perceptions. The feedback we receive confirms our initial expectations, thereby promoting similar behaviors in the future. After a series of similar experiences, the self-concept begins to "solidify" to the point that we become what we expected to be. We all have self-concepts that were developed in a large part by the feedback we received from others.

But this book is about your academic future, not your academic past. The point is not just that the self-fulfilling prophecy explains how you became the way you are; even more important, it holds a powerful message for you today: *You can use the very same process to your advantage to change yourself, to change both the way you see yourself as a student and the way you perform in the classroom. You can become a different student, and you can start today.*

> If [today's students] can conceive it and believe it, they can achieve it. They must know it is not their aptitude but their attitude that will determine their altitude.
>
> JESSE JACKSON

Recreating Yourself

To change some facet of yourself as a student, you have to begin with the belief that you can change. Forget what you have heard about old dogs not learning new tricks and leopards not changing their spots. There are almost certainly hundreds of students walking your campus who are living proof that people can become more competent and successful students. Here's how.

1 Put yourself in situations where you can experience success.

The whole process requires that you be able to create a cycle of success, so it's important that you choose the right starting place. You must put the issue of will and determination aside for a moment and be realistic. In our first scenario of Jennifer, in which she arrives at college deficient in math skills, the strongest will and most positive attitude in the world probably wouldn't help her if she tries to start her math work with calculus. If she wants to become a more competent math student, she has to start in a class that will challenge her enough to make her success meaningful, but still offer her a reasonable chance of succeeding. As the previous section noted, self-fulfilling prophecies begin with the "planting" of an expectation. Don't make the mistake of programming yourself for failure by creating an unreasonable expectation.

2 Set specific goals.

You have to start the process with a specific set of objectives, not vague hopes such as "I want to do well in my biology class" or "I want to go to class often enough so that my teacher won't drop me." You will be better off by setting goals that are specific and measurable: "I want to make at least a B in biology class" or "I want to make at least a 90 on my next biology exam" or "I want to make it through this class with no more than three absences."

Specific goals give you a clear focus and make it possible to measure your progress in meaningful ways. Make a point of stating these goals formally and writing them down.

3 Seek out those who can give you positive, honest feedback.

Just as you didn't develop your existing self-concept in isolation, you can't change it in isolation, either. You will need the feedback of others to help you develop competence. In some cases, this may require that you distance yourself physically or psychologically from those who have known you as unsuccessful, or perhaps even contributed to your seeing yourself as unsuccessful. If you want to become a better student, "rub elbows" with better students. Interact with those who are themselves trying to be successful. You might start this process simply by moving from the back row of the classroom or those areas outside the center of classroom involvement to more conspicuous locations toward front and center. If you live in a dorm, find someone on your floor who is making a clear commitment to being successful, and try to strike up a friendship.

A member of the faculty or staff at your institution can play a valuable role in helping to shape a new impression of yourself as a student. Make an effort to strike up a relationship with one or more faculty members or counselors who send out positive, upbeat messages in class or in their informal interactions with students. Seek out someone on campus who challenges you and expects a lot out of you. If such a person can serve as an informal mentor and play the important role of providing you encouragement and realistic feedback, that individual can help ensure your success.

4 Turn failures into learning experiences.

People often scoff at those with sunny dispositions who quote trite expressions such as "When life gives you lemons, make lemonade" or "Turn your stumbling blocks into stepping stones." But the truth remains that we can learn valuable lessons from mistakes and failures. As noted in a later chapter, we won't always see a nice, unbroken line of progress when we look at our growth in college. There will be setbacks and occasional backsliding. While none of us enjoys getting back a poor test score, such a test holds a wealth of information; if nothing else, it lets us know what strategies in a class are *not* working. Sometimes we have to stop and honestly assess our behavior, asking ourselves, "How did I manage to choose failure here? What old habits am I still clinging to? How do I need to change? What could I do to make sure this doesn't happen again?"

People change and forget to tell each other.

LILLIAN HELLMAN

The way I see it, if you want the rainbow, you gotta put up with the rain.

DOLLY PARTON

5 Accept success.

One of the most difficult tasks ahead of us is to accept success gracefully. Many students suffer from what some educators refer to as the "impostor syndrome." Such students see themselves as impostors: "I'm not a *real* student, not capable like everyone else in the class. Sure, I made a pretty good test score, but maybe I got lucky or the professor just decided to be kind on this test. Surely the teacher will sooner or later see right through me." The whole point of this process of recreating yourself is to try to create a positive self-fulfilling prophecy. Put yourself into a situation where you can be successful, plan how that success can take place, be responsive to those who offer positive feedback, and accept the success when it comes. Many of us have very persistent "scripts" for failure, expectations that go back many years. When success does come, we have to accept it and see how we can continue to be successful in the future.

As you begin to rummage around in your *Toolkit for College Success,* you will encounter some new ideas that perhaps won't fit into the way you currently see yourself and the educational process. Try to be open to these ideas and the tools and strategies this book offers to you. But most of all, as you turn the next page, do so with the expectation that you *can* attain success in college.

Of all the traps and pitfalls of life, self-disesteem is the deadliest, and the hardest to overcome, for it is a pit designed and dug by our own hands, summed up in the phrase, "It's no use—I can't do it."

MAXWELL MALTZ

We were born to improvise ourselves as human beings.

BUTTERFLY MCQUEEN

Chapter 2

Life is what happens to you while you're busy making other plans.

JOHN LENNON (1940–1980)

Planning

Managing

for Success

Time and Materials

Dost thou love life? Then do not squander
Time; for that's the Stuff Life is made of.

BENJAMIN FRANKLIN (1706–1790)

Managing Essential Student Resources: Time and Materials

Casey is what people in education call a "traditional" college freshman. He is eighteen and just graduated from high school the preceding May. To make sure he can adjust to college life, he has decided not to overload his first semester schedule. Casey is enrolled in fourteen credit hours: freshman composition, history, speech, biology, and physical education. His parents have insisted that he not work his first semester. After four years of high school, in which every hour of every class day was structured and tightly scheduled, Casey is pleased to discover that he will spend only a total of about sixteen hours in class and lab each week, or just about three hours a day. Noting that this amount of class time is less than half of what he has grown accustomed to through his high school years, Casey ponders what looks like a pleasant schedule. He calculates that he will have time just about every day to head back to the dorm for a nap after his morning classes. He decides that he will like the pace of life on a college campus.

Carmen doesn't fit the mold of the traditional college freshman, though students like her are a fast-growing part of the college population. She is twenty-eight, married, and has an eight-year-old daughter. Carmen has spent the last couple of years working as a legal secretary, and she has been encouraged by both the law firm and her husband to start her college work. Luckily, she will be allowed to continue working about twenty hours a week to help pay for her college costs, and she lives about thirty minutes away from the university in which she has just enrolled for her first semester. She has taken a conservative course load of ten credit hours, knowing that she will be challenged to meet the demands of a family, part-time job, and her course work.

Which of these two students has the greater challenge in time management? Most people would say the obvious answer is Carmen. Her life promises to be much more hectic and demanding than Casey's. But actually both people have a potential problem. Whereas Carmen will have to manage time wisely just to be able to function as a wife, mother, secretary, and student, Casey's challenge will be in managing a surplus of time. When a student has what appears to be a great deal of free time, it becomes easy to put off work that needs to be done on a day-to-day basis, to develop lax study and work habits, or to delay starting major projects. *Both* Carmen and Casey will need to manage time wisely to prosper in their freshman year.

Students must also learn to manage materials wisely. College students can quickly become weighed down with textbooks, lab manuals, as well as a variety of handouts, printed materials, and returned assignments that will grow over the semester. Soon their desks and lives are so cluttered that they face almost daily frustration finding the notes they need to study for an exam, the English paper they typed yesterday (and that's due in ten minutes!), or some other misplaced treasure.

Time and materials are two of the most valuable commodities students have. Like anything of value, these commodities are limited and must be managed if students are to function successfully in an academic setting.

Time Shares

It may be helpful to carry our comparison of time as a commodity a bit further. The value of time, of course, is that it has a limited number of "shares"—only 24 hours in a day. Sometimes we "spend" time in ways that are very satisfying to us; at other times, we "give" of our time or perhaps have it "stolen" away by others.

The first step in learning to manage your time is to see where it's going now. How do you invest the 24 hours a day and 168 hours you have each week? It may be helpful to look at time as being shared among three main categories of "investments": required activities, schedules activities, and discretionary activities.

Required Activities

Each of us must invest a portion of our time shares in activities that maintain our health and certain important relationships. Some required activities are purely physical; each of us needs to spend a certain number of hours sleeping and eating, for example. Other required activities satisfy emotional needs. Some tasks are required to maintain our relationships with those most important to

us. Parents and spouses must devote an amount of time and attention to fulfilling their responsibilities to other family members. (Carmen, for instance, can't stop being a wife and mother to reach her goal of becoming a student.) While we sometimes need to negotiate assertively on the amount, we need to allot some time to support these important relationships. Therefore, each of us must devote a portion of our day to meeting our own basic human needs and those of others, but we often have some latitude about the specific times we carry out these activities.

Scheduled Activities

Another block of time shares must be devoted to certain other activities that we have a commitment to perform. Unlike required activities, these typically occur at regular and predictable times. For example, Casey knows that he is expected to be in class and labs at certain hours. Carmen has to schedule twenty hours of work each week at the law firm. She also has to spend time commuting to and from her classes at the university. We all make commitments to other important activities: dental appointments, club meetings, church activities, and so on. Scheduled activities are only a little less important than our required activities, but they can be demanding because they usually must occur at specific times.

Discretionary Activities

Time is truly the great enemy. It's not the great healer, it's the great stealer.

Sylvester Stallone

The final block of time shares is for discretionary activities. They are not so urgent that failing to perform them *on a particular day* threatens our well-being or the requirements of a role we play. Some, however, are important enough that we cannot afford to overlook them completely. Obviously, out-of-class study and learning activities collectively fall into this category. Many other day-to-day activities fit into this group: grooming, household activities, social interactions, phone conversations, television time, and a variety of other leisure activities. Discretionary activities are the most flexible; we can schedule them *when* we want and *if* we want.

Consider for a moment Casey and Carmen. How are they investing their time shares? Casey probably has limited required activities. He has to sleep and eat like everyone else, but his family commitments aren't great on a day-to-day basis. He is committed to sixteen hours of class and lab time each week for his scheduled activities but has few other such commitments. He has a wealth of shares that he can invest in discretionary activities. The danger he faces is having so much time that he stops valuing it and seeing any need for managing it at all.

Carmen has to devote a lot of her shares to required and scheduled activities balanced among the roles she plays as worker, student, wife, and mother. Her challenge is finding or making time for her discretionary activities, both for study time and for time to devote to herself and the leisure activities she needs to lead a balanced life.

It may help you visualize how students invest their time shares by representing these ideas graphically. **Templates 2.1 and 2.2** on the following pages illustrate how Casey and Carmen spend their time. Think of the columns on the page as being like the graduated cylinders you might have used in a science class. Each cylinder has room for only twenty-four time shares. The cylinder on the left of each figure represents how Casey and Carmen spend most of their weekdays. The other two cylinders in each figure show how Casey and Carmen use time on a typical Saturday and Sunday.

As you can see, these portfolios reflect the challenges both these freshmen face in managing their time. Carmen's discretionary time is very limited on weekdays, so she has chosen to concentrate her study time on Sunday. What suggestions might you make to help her improve her use of time? Casey, by contrast, has a great deal of discretionary time on his hands. Nevertheless, he spends only a little more time each week in support of his classwork than does Carmen. Casey needs to rethink his commitment to time he spends on out-of-class study. Perhaps he needs to make the mental shift to move study time into the scheduled category. If he can discipline himself to block out more time for coursework and schedule it so that it becomes a routine activity, he will be well on his way to becoming a better time manager.

How about you? How do you invest your time in these categories? The first step in becoming a better time manager is to see where your time goes now. The tool section beginning on page 20 will help you see how you invest your allotment of 168 time shares each week.

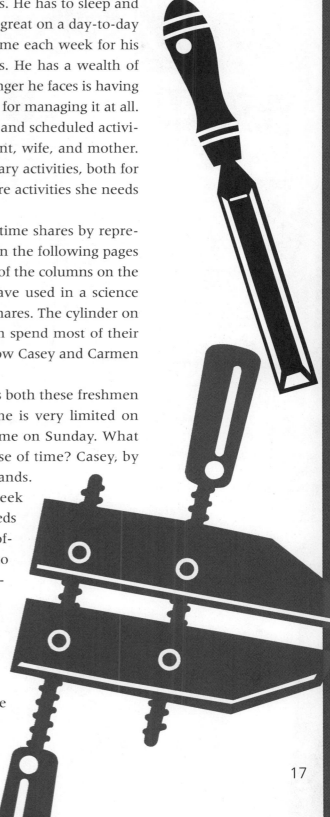

Getting a Measure of Time
Casey's Time Portfolio

Weekdays

Leisure/Social
Leisure/Social
Leisure/Social
Study
Study
Study
Sports/Exercise
TV
TV
Grooming
Lab
Class Time
Class Time
Class Time
Meals
Meals
Sleep
Sleep
Sleep
Sleep
Sleep
Sleep
Sleep
Sleep

Saturday

Leisure/Social
Leisure/Social
Leisure/Social
Leisure/Social
Leisure/Social
Leisure/Social
Leisure/Social
TV
TV
Sports/Exercise
Sports/Exercise
Sports/Exercise
Grooming
Meals
Meals
Sleep
Sleep
Sleep
Sleep
Sleep
Sleep
Sleep
Sleep

Sunday

Leisure/Social
Leisure/Social
Leisure/Social
Leisure/Social
Leisure/Social
Study
Study
Study
TV
TV
Sports/Exercise
Sports/Exercise
Grooming
Church
Church
Meals
Meals
Sleep
Sleep
Sleep
Sleep
Sleep
Sleep

Weekdays
Required Hours _____ 10 _____
Scheduled Hours _____ 4 _____
Discretionary Hours _____ 10 _____

Saturday
Required Hours _____ 11 _____
Scheduled Hours _____ 0 _____
Discretionary Hours _____ 13 _____

Sunday
Required Hours _____ 9 _____
Scheduled Hours _____ 2 _____
Discretionary Hours _____ 13 _____

Getting a Measure of Time
Carmen's Time Portfolio

Weekdays	Saturday	Sunday
Leisure/TV	Leisure/Social	Leisure/Social
Study	Leisure/Social	Leisure/Social
Study	Leisure/Social	Leisure/Social
Housework	Leisure/Social	Leisure/Social
Grooming	Grooming	Study
Work	Shopping	Study
Work	Shopping	Study
Work	Housework	Study
Work	Housework	Study
Commuting	Housework	Grooming
Class Time/Commuting	Housework	Housework
Class Time	Family Time	Housework
Class Time	Family Time	Family Time
Family Time	Family Time	Family Time
Family Time	Meals	Family Time
Meals	Meals	Meals
Meals	Sleep	Meals
Meals	Sleep	Sleep
Sleep	Sleep	Sleep
Sleep	Sleep	Sleep
Sleep	Sleep	Sleep
Sleep	Sleep	Sleep
Sleep	Sleep	Sleep
Sleep	Sleep	

Weekdays		Saturday		Sunday	
Required Hours	11	Required Hours	13	Required Hours	12
Scheduled Hours	8	Scheduled Hours	0	Scheduled Hours	0
Discretionary Hours	5	Discretionary Hours	11	Discretionary Hours	12

Your Time Portfolio

Let's see how you cash in your time shares each week. **Template 2.3** will help you get a fairly accurate measurement of how you spend your time. It is important to be as honest as possible in this exercise: consider how you actually *do* use time, not how you *should be* using time.

The column farthest to the left represents a "typical" weekday. Though your days may vary somewhat according to your specific school and work schedule, you need to determine an average that is typical for each weekday. To fill in this first column, count the total number of hours devoted each week to required and scheduled activities, and divide by 5. The next two columns are for Saturdays and Sundays. Again, to fill in these columns you need to consider how you typically spend time on weekends.

To fill out the template and get an idea of how you invest your time, follow these steps:

1. Using a pencil and starting at the bottom of each "graduated cylinder," fill in the amounts of time you *actually spend* in the activities that are required for you to maintain your health and to meet the essential needs of those who depend on you. This is time you spend sleeping, eating, satisfying special medical needs, and so on. It also includes the amount of time you devote to caring for others. Label the hour blocks to reflect how this time is spent: for example, seven hours sleeping, three hours preparing and/or eating meals, two hours of essential family time, and so on. When you are finished filling in the required activity hours, draw a bold line across the cylinder to mark where this category stops.

2. Next, continue filling in the cylinders with the time you spend in a typical weekday and on the weekends in scheduled activities: class and lab time, work, commuting time, and other regular, predictable commitments. Once again, draw a bold line across the cylinder to mark where this category stops.

3. Next, consider the amount of "room" you have at the top of each cylinder for discretionary activities. Does it look accurate? Consider how much time in a day you have left over for discretionary activities: school work and study, leisure activity, grooming time, television time, reading, talking on the phone, housework, running errands, and so on. Remember—just as in real life, it all has to fit into twenty-four hours! You may need to make minor adjustments in the three main categories, but work with the time shares until the columns look accurate. Write the totals for the three categories of activities at the bottom of each column.

4. Finally, take a good, close look at the category totals. What do they tell you about the way you are currently using time? Compare your totals to those of your classmates. Since our immediate concern is improving your study skills and learning, figure out how much discretionary time is available to you, particularly on weekdays, to devote to reading, reviewing, homework, and other such activities. What discretionary activities gobble up most of this time block? Do you have greater freedom on the weekends to make up for a lack of discretionary time during the week? Can you move some activities from one category to another, or perhaps negotiate with family members to take on some of the tasks currently tying you up and robbing time that you need to apply to schoolwork?

Getting a Measure of Time

Weekdays	Saturday	Sunday

Required Hours   _____

Scheduled Hours   _____

Discretionary Hours   _____

Required Hours   _____

Scheduled Hours   _____

Discretionary Hours   _____

Required Hours   _____

Scheduled Hours   _____

Discretionary Hours   _____

The template exercise should open your eyes to the need to make decisions about how you use time. The "tips" section below offers some suggestions to make the most of your time.

Five Tips for Making Time

Although it is technically impossible to "make" any more time, here are some fairly simple strategies that can help you free up extra time.

1 CARRY "POCKET TASKS" WITH YOU AT ALL TIMES.

Most of us are wasteful of little blocks of time that are like transition periods between our larger tasks. Perhaps your government teacher dismissed class about ten minutes early, your carpool partner is running a few minutes late, the dental hygienist you are scheduled to see at 1:00 PM is running a little late on her lunch break, and so on. We tend to fritter away such blocks of time, which are in fact ideal for certain study activities. In five or ten minutes, you could review the sociology chapter you read last night. You could pull out of your purse or pocket some note cards that you constructed to help you learn terms for your botany test on Friday. It would be just enough time to preview the government chapter you will need to tackle later this evening. Don't be caught without something to do when a few free minutes come your way. Carry pocket tasks with you for just such opportunities.

2 ON BIG TASKS, DIVIDE AND CONQUER.

Many students have problems getting started on the major tasks they have to do: research assignments, lab projects, term papers, and so on. The sheer size of such a task can be intimidating, but closer analysis reveals that it isn't a singular "mega-task." All such jobs are really a collection of many individual tasks. You should approach these major projects by seeing how you can break them down into a number of smaller tasks that could each be accomplished in thirty to forty-five minutes or so. Over a period of time, you can schedule the dozen or so resulting tasks into your daily schedules just like any other activities.

On major tasks, it may be advisable to make out a flowchart to help you think through the main steps or phases you will need to accomplish. A tool sheet illustrating the process of flowcharting follows later in the chapter.

3 SCHEDULE YOUR STUDY TIME IN YOUR "PRIME-TIME" SLOT.

Most people have a sense that they function better at certain times of the day. "Morning people" are early risers and have no problems getting up and charging ahead into the day. They may do their best work before lunch. Others start the day a little slower and may be at their mental peak in the afternoon. "Night owls" feel that they function best in the evening. Your prime time is both a function of your internal clock and the nature of your schedule. After doing the time shares exercise, you may be in a position to determine that there are blocks in your day when you need to schedule your study time to make the most of your efforts. Don't make study time the last activity of the day if you hit your mental peak hours earlier. Determine when you are at your best and try to juggle your schedule to allow for at least some study time during your prime-time slot.

> I long to accomplish a great and noble task, but it is my chief duty to accomplish small tasks as if they were great and noble.
>
> HELEN KELLER

4 NEGOTIATE ASSERTIVELY WITH OTHERS WHO CLAIM SOME OF YOUR TIME SHARES.

When you did the time shares exercise, you may have been a little surprised at how much of your time is shared with others. As we noted earlier in the chapter, most of us have a responsibility to devote a certain amount of our time to maintain relationships with those who are most important to us. But beyond what fits into the "required" activities, how much of our scheduled and discretionary time can we devote to others and still reach the goals we have set for ourselves? In Carmen's case, she may need to talk to her husband about sharing more of the day-to-day housework or child care. She may be able to set up an hour or so of routine "homework time" that she can share with her daughter each weekday, when both can work quietly on schoolwork. If her weekdays are just too crowded, she can talk to her employer and see whether she can readjust her schedule or perhaps work a few hours on week-

ends. Carmen may want to lay claim to several hours of time during the weekend and encourage her husband and daughter to make that a regular time when the two of them could be out of the house for some sort of special outing together. If Carmen can get her family to accept and support her plans to get an education, they can then work together to restructure the daily routines of life to allow for her need for study time. Time is a negotiable asset, and sometimes we must be assertive and creative in our relationships with others to help us manage our time together.

5 MAKE A COMMITMENT TO BUDGETING YOUR TIME ON A REGULAR BASIS.

The best overall strategy for improving your use of time is to budget it the same way you do any other scarce commodity. People forced to live on a limited income often see the need to make out a weekly or monthly budget. This activity is essential to making sure that money will be there when it's needed to pay for the essentials of life. Most effective money managers begin the budgeting process by identifying the important fixed expenses. Once those are covered, the remaining money can be parceled out to

less essential expenses, and then to leisure and luxury expenses. You have to approach the task of managing time the same way. You begin by identifying your fixed needs—the required and scheduled activities. Once you allow time for those, you can turn your attention to discretionary activities, with some sense of setting priorities to determine which are relatively important and which represent "time luxury items."

You can greatly improve how you manage your time by using weekly overviews and daily time plans. The following tool and template sections offer some guidelines to help you improve the way you budget and spend your time.

Time Budgeting

Some people resist the notion of scheduling time because they fear the practice will turn them into some sort of robot, living out each day according to a rigid program they have created for themselves. But the truth of the matter is that if we go about the task rationally, we can make our lives *less* hurried. By making a few simple decisions regarding our priorities, we can actually free up more time for leisure or social activities. For the Carmens of the world, budgeting time on a regular basis is a survival strategy—time is so precious that it must be budgeted carefully. For the Caseys, who on the surface are time-wealthy, budgeting helps establish important study routines and prevents procrastination.

You can take a major step toward better management of your time by using "A Student's Week at a Glance" template. **Templates 2.4** and **2.5** on pages 27 and 28 show how Casey and Carmen might budget their time during a week of classes. Class time and scheduled activities are listed on the left side of the page, and a "to do" list is on the right.

The key to effective time planning is to keep the system simple and workable. The following steps should help you develop a system that can work for you.

1 Use a monthly calendar to keep track of important dates and assignments.

You can buy an inexpensive monthly calendar that is designed to fit in a standard notebook. Use the calendar to record major assignment due dates, test dates, meetings, and other formal appointments.

2 Begin the week by filling out "A Student's Week at a Glance."

Template 2.6 on page 29 is blank; you can use it to manage your time shares wisely. Sometime during the weekend, try to get an overview of the important activities scheduled for the week ahead. Do this *before* Monday morning; once the week begins, it is easy to put off doing it at all. Find some quiet time on the weekend, and with the help of the notes you have on your monthly calendar, list scheduled activities, meetings, appointments, tests, and so on, in the Monday through Friday blocks on the left side of the page. In the "to do" column, list the discretionary tasks that you can identify. These are nonscheduled, nonroutine tasks that you will need to accomplish during the week. Such activities might include work you need to do on assignments, review periods for exams, research for a library project, or a variety of other tasks that fall outside the scope of your college work: getting your automobile license tags renewed, shopping for a gift for a friend, and so on. Simply write down such "to do" tasks as they occur to you.

3 Establish daily priorities for items on your "to do" list.

You need to consider the relative importance of tasks on your "to do" list and assign a priority rating for each. It is essential that you do this step on a routine basis. You may find that evening is the best time to establish priorities for the following day, or, if you are an early riser, you can establish priorities as part of your morning routine.

In the column marked "priority," use code letters to mark tasks according to their urgency. Items that are both urgent and important should be given the code letter *A*. These are tasks that need to be done within the next twenty-four-hour period. Consider the tasks carefully, and give an *A*-ranking only to those important items that need to be done *today*. Tasks that are important but not urgent are given the code letter *B*. If you have the time to do so, you may want to tackle these tasks within the next twenty-four hours, but it is not essential that they be done right away. Tasks that are neither particularly urgent nor important are given letter *C* priority ratings. These are activities that you may choose to do if your schedule is light: pick up some clothes at the cleaners, start reading a novel you will need to write about in several weeks, and so on.

4 Follow the cardinal rule of time planning: when you have time to devote to discretionary tasks, work first on *A*-priority activities.

This is the key to effective use of time: *devote the time you have for discretionary activities only to A-priority tasks, until all such tasks are completed*. Don't start a B- or a C-level task if any A-items are on your list. Do the urgent and important things first. Whatever time is left over you can then use to tackle other less urgent tasks or for leisure or social activities. (There is nothing wrong with spending some of your day in such "unimportant" activities. That's the whole purpose of time management: to do the things you *must* do so that you free up time to do the things you *like* to do.)

5 Update your "to do" list daily.

As you accomplish tasks, strike them off your list. (It will be very satisfying to see this list of deleted items grow throughout the week!) As new tasks arise, add them to the list, and as a part of your daily planning routine, update the priority rating for items on the list. Items that you rated B or even C on Monday may become A-tasks by Thursday or Friday. Simply update the list as the week rolls along and keep your focus on A-level activities.

That's it! Time planning doesn't have to be a complex chore. The key is to make it a routine activity. Next, let's consider how you might use a process called flowcharting to help you plan more complex tasks.

A Student's Week at a Glance *(Casey)*

For week of September 28

Scheduled Activities	To do	Priority
M Class 9–11	Do research on speech topic	B
	Write causal analysis draft	B
	Buy and mail Dad's birthday card	A
T Class 8–11 Botany lab 1–3:30 Class 6–9	Check out book from history reading list	B
	Read chapter 4 in history text	A
	Pay car insurance!	A
W Class 9–11 Intramural Flag Football game 3:00 pm	Study for botany lab quiz	A
	Wash car	C
Th Class 8–11 History study group in Library 1:00 pm	Make appointment w/ Financial Aid counselor	B
F Class 9–11		

A Student's Week at a Glance (Carmen)

For week of September 28

Scheduled Activities	To do	Priority
M Class 8–10 Work 12–4 Chem Lab 6–8:30	Study for Psych. test	A
	Read Chapter 3 in chemistry text	A
	Help Catherine w/ church newsletter	B
T Class 8–9:30 Work 12–4 Aerobics class 6–7	Call Lori about car pooling	C
	Drop off stuff at recycling center	C
	Pick up paint from hardware store	B
W Class 8–10 Conference w/Rachel's teacher 11–11:30 Work 12–4	Shop for groceries	B
	Take Rachel shopping for jeans	B
	Go by Dr. Peterson's office about last test	B
Th Class 8–9:30 Dental Appt. 10:00 Work 12–4 Aerobics class 6–7	Read chapter 5 in Psych. book	A
F Class 8–10 Work 12–4		

A Student's Week at a Glance
For week of

SEE OTHER SIDE FOR DIRECTIONS

Scheduled Activities	To do	Priority
M		
T		
W		
Th		
F		

Directions for Template 2.6

1. In a period of quiet time during the weekend, start by listing scheduled activities (classes, work hours, meetings, formal appointments, and so on) in the appropriate blocks on the left side of the template. Be sure to consult your monthly calendar for special events.

2. Next, in the "to do" column, list the discretionary tasks that you need to accomplish. These are *unscheduled, nonroutine* tasks. (Do not include routine activities like preparing meals, grooming activities, driving to work or school, and so on). Your "to do" list should reflect study time, homework assignments, and a variety of personal tasks that you need to get done.

3. Rate each item on the "to do" list you have created: *A* for important and urgent tasks, *B* for important but nonurgent tasks, and *C* for tasks that are neither urgent nor important.

4. When you have discretionary time at your disposal, focus your attention on the *A*-rated tasks. Do your best to accomplish these tasks before you attempt any tasks rated *B* or *C*. *Your basic objective is to complete all of the A tasks.* After your *A* tasks are completed, you may choose to do tasks rated *B* or *C*. Cross tasks off the list when you complete them.

5. In a quiet period each day, add to the list new tasks that you have identified, and update the priority ratings of the remaining tasks as their importance or urgency changes.

2. *A monthly calendar* These can be purchased as loose-leaf inserts to fit in a standard notebook. You will use the calendar to record important due dates, meetings, holidays, and other activities typically scheduled more than a week or so in advance.

3. *Pocket divider* Purchase sturdy pocket dividers, one for each course you are taking. Use them to separate the notebook into easily identifiable subject sections and to help you keep up with handouts, returned tests, and assignments you are ready to turn in.

4. *Course Data Sheet* You can use **Template 2.7** to create a valuable record of important information relating to each class: the time and location of the class, the teacher's name, office number, required textbooks, major assignments, grading formula, and so on. The filled-out Course Data Sheet should be the first page in each subject section. **Template 2.8** is blank for your use.

5. *Assignment Log* Over the semester, you need to keep track of formal assignments, as well as any of the grades you make on these assignments and on exams. **Template 2.9** shows you how you can use the "Assignment Log" to keep a record of your work. Include an Assignment Log sheet in each subject section in your notebook, and get into the routine of recording assignments on the sheet at the conclusion of each class. **Template 2.10** is blank for your use.

6. *I-Note pages* Chapter 4 introduces you to this valuable note-taking format. You can make copies of the templates or construct your own. For each subject section, include a supply of these pages for in-class note taking.

7. *High quality, standard-rule notebook paper* You might want to put a supply of this paper in the back of your notebook so that you will have it for in-class written work.

You may wish to add other devices to meet your own needs. Velcro can be used to attach pens or pencils, and a variety of Post-It notes might be handy to have for special reminders you need to create for yourself. You will also probably want to get a hole-punch so that you can easily insert handouts your instructors provide for you.

As the semester passes, you may discover that your three-ring survival kit is getting pretty bulky. You may need to pull out old materials and keep them in folders for possible reference later. But give this all-in-one notebook a try. A loose-leaf system makes it easier for you to keep up with materials and can help you improve your study habits, as you will see in Chapter 4.

Course Data Sheet

COURSE TITLE

General Psychology

MEETING TIME

8:10–9 MWF

LOCATION

Evans Hall 210

INSTRUCTOR

Dr. Ruth Pratt

INSTRUCTOR'S OFFICE

Evans Hall 216C

OFFICE HOURS

9–11, 2–3 MWF
12–2 T TH

TEXTBOOKS

Introduction to Psychology

GRADING FORMULA

Quizzes - (4) - 40%   Mid-Semester Exam - 20%
Self-Analysis - 10%   Final Exam - 20%
Group Project - 10%

MAJOR TESTS/ASSIGNMENTS	DATE DUE
	October 18
Group Project	November 15
Self-Analysis	October 27
Mid-Semester Exam	December 17
Final Exam	

Course Data Sheet

SEE OTHER SIDE FOR DIRECTIONS

COURSE TITLE

INSTRUCTOR

MEETING TIME

INSTRUCTOR'S OFFICE

LOCATION

OFFICE HOURS

TEXTBOOKS

GRADING FORMULA

MAJOR TESTS/ASSIGNMENTS	DATE DUE

Directions for Template 2.8

1. Fill in the appropriate boxes, based on information you receive from your instructor at the beginning of the semester. Some of this information may be listed in the course syllabus or handouts.

2. Place this page at the beginning of each subject section of your notebook, immediately after the pocket divider.

3. If your instructor announces due dates for major assignments or tests, transfer these to your monthly calendar or "Week at a Glance" pages.

Assignment Log for Botany

Assignment	DUE DATE	DATE TURNED IN	GRADE
Read Chapter 2	9-15		
Read Chapter 3 - pp 47–60	9-17		
Lab Quiz 1	9-17		90
Finish Chapter 3 - pp 60–72	9-22		
Read Chapter 4	9-24		
Exam 1 (Chs 2–4)	9-29		77
Read Chapter 5	10-1		
Read Chapter 7	10-6		
Lab Quiz 2	10-8		85
Read Chapter 8	10-8		
Exam 2 (Chs 5, 7, 8)	10-13		85
Read Chapter 9	10-15		
Lab Quiz 3	10-15		100
Read Chapter 10	10-20		
Mid-Semester exam (Chs 2–5, 7–10)	10-27		90!
Read Chapter 11	10-29		
Lab Quiz 4	10-29		

Assignment Log for

SEE OTHER SIDE FOR DIRECTIONS

Assignment	DUE DATE	DATE TURNED IN	GRADE

Directions for Template 2.10

1. Record assignments in the log when the instructor gives them.

2. Record test and assignment grades when work is returned.

3. Transfer data from this template to your "Week at a Glance" sheet to help you plan time for assignments.

Notes

Chapter 3

Connecting

Getting Results

*F*rom your parents you learn love and laughter

and how to put one foot in front of the other.

But when books are opened you discover that

you have wings.

HELEN HAYES (1900–1993)

with the Text

from Your Reading

If you would be a reader, read....

EPICTETUS (C. 55–135 A.D.)

'Tis the good reader that makes the good book....

RALPH WALDO EMERSON (1803–1882)

Some Reflections on Reading

This chapter does not presume to teach you how to read. You already know how to do that. But most students have never approached the process of reading from the perspective of understanding what happens when reading takes place and what practices might be useful to make reading textbook assignments an easier and more fruitful activity. That's what this chapter is all about.

In this theory section, our concern is to develop a better grasp of the process of reading. We can begin by focusing on some new perspectives on the reading process.

Reading Principles

1 We become better readers by reading.

Many people are under the impression that reading improvement comes from learning "tricks" or mastering some mechanical gimmicks that will magically improve reading speed and comprehension. However, most reading professionals agree that we learn to read better simply as a result of reading widely. So much of reading depends on our "prior knowledge"—that information that we carry inside our head when we open the page and begin reading. Many learning theorists maintain that we remember new information only if we relate it to knowledge we already hold. There is no greater guarantee of a person's reading efficiency than extensive experience with words on the printed page. You can make slow but steady progress as a reader simply by reading more extensively to increase your base of knowledge.

2 More than anything else, reading is a process of predicting.

If you were to pick up a book, turn to the first page, and read the line, "Once upon a time, in a magical land and a magical time…" your mind automatically begins to make predictions: "This is a fairy tale or fable of some kind…some of the characters will be 'bad' and others will be 'good.' There will probably be a happy ending, and the story will teach a simple little lesson…." and so on. As we actively read, our mind is always racing ahead of where our eyes are on the page, wondering, speculating, predicting, and then eventually either confirming

> *Reading is a means of thinking with another person's mind: it forces you to stretch your own.*
>
> CHARLES SCRIBNER JR.

those predictions that ... were not accurate. (In under-... a process of predicting ... you are well under way to ... comprehension and ... reading rate in text reading ... the "tools" section of ... this chapter.)

those predictions or correcting ...
standing that reading is largely a ...
learning how to improve your ...
assignments, as you will see in the "tools" section ...

3 Reading is an interactive process, not a passive one.

Many students are under the impression that reading is a "laid-back" activity—that the mind is some sort of sponge that soaks up meaning as the eyes move across the page. Effective readers are usually involved—questioning, probing, analyzing, disagreeing, doubting, or in some other way *reacting to* the words on the page.

Because reading is an interactive process, we must treat it differently ... we do for leisure ... entertainment. You may be able to take a ... novel to your bed ... comfortable pillow under your head, and ... and still stay fo ... may even have a radio going in the back- ... textbook, ... book. Using the same strategy with your ... your reading efficiency ... to disaster. You may find that you can read ... mental activity it is and ... if you put yourself in a different environ- ... posture that will better ... able, or your desk. Read sitting straight up ... environment with a minimum of distractions.

If you tre **slightly above** put yo...

... of the same ... ting its size, ... llustrations, ... survey- ... late the ... topic.

... supper mental activities, we ... mental potential when ... lapse into a nice com- ... eps the mind busy and ... y our surroundings or ... ed to the task of read- ... ed to believe that they ... down, but that advice ... will "drive better" if ... miles per hour on an ... w driver is prone to ... cenery, may become ... pace, or perhaps will ... teresting, pursuits, such as ... cs equalizer on the car stereo ... thus becomes only one of the ... mpeting for the driver's attention. ... will probably do a better job of reading ... press yourself to read 10 percent or so ... bove your typical rate, just enough to require your mind to stay alert and focused. (You are probably capable of reading 30 or 40 percent faster with some effort, but the point is not to make reading a frenzied activity—just a focused one.)

SRSR:
Four Steps to Better
Reading

SRSR is ~~a~~ tool employing four steps that ~~will~~ dramatically improve your comprehension and re~~tention~~ of reading assignments. In the first step—*survey*—~~you ex~~plore the passage you are to read, sampling its co~~ntent~~ ~~so~~ ~~th~~e ~~th~~at will help you make predictions abou~~t~~ ~~~~ ~~re~~ ~~the~~ the information to your prior knowledge ~~~~ ~~~~ the passage to understand its main ideas an~~d~~ ~~and~~ ~~sub~~ the expectations you created in the first ste~~p.~~ ~~read~~ you identify the key points in the chapter and ~~~~ ~~sub~~ ~~read~~ is easy to review. The final step—*reflect*—helps ~~you~~ learned, making it less likely that the informatio~~n~~ ~~~~ ~~ting bou~~ working memory. ~~helps~~

Survey

Consider for a moment what a surveyor does. A surveyo~~r~~ aries of a piece of property, noting its significant physica~~l~~ slope, and so on, all for the purpose of clearly understandi~~ng~~ establishing its position in relationship to other known poi~~nts~~ marks, as well as to other known properties.

In surveying an unfamiliar passage, you should have ma~~ny~~ objectives. You should attempt to get a measure of the passage, ~~its~~ topic, and scope. By scanning headings, short passages of text, and i~~~~ you will develop a sense of the passage's tone and structure. All of the~~se~~ ing efforts provide an overview of the material and help you begin to r~~elate~~ material to the mental "benchmarks" of your prior knowledge on that~~~~

The surveying process should include the following steps:

1 Reading the introduction and summary sections of the chapter.

▬ Many textbook authors provide introductions and summaries set off from the main text of the chapter. Others list specific learning objectives on the chapter's title page. If the passage does not have a formal introduction, summary, or objective statements, quickly scan the first and last page of the passage.

2 Noting the chapter title, headings, and subheadings.

▬ The chapter title identifies the main topic of the chapter and often suggests a tone or attitude toward the material. The headings and subheadings are usually clearly identified by distinct print styles and sizes, as well as by other markers such as

boxes, underlining, and special typesetting marks called "bullets." The headings and subheadings typically reflect the overall structure of the work: the main headings label the passage's main ideas, and the subheadings label subdivisions or important supporting ideas. The headings and subheadings establish the "skeleton" of the work. Just as a paleontologist can tell a great deal about a prehistoric creature from an unearthed fossil skeleton, you can begin to form an image in your head of the passage according to the skeleton revealed by the surveying process.

As you take in these headings and subheadings, you can quickly scan short sections of the textual material as an aid to clarifying what each of the headings or subheadings deals with.

3 Examining illustrations or other supporting material.

Many authors include pictures, graphs, charts, cartoons, and other supporting material to help develop their ideas. As you survey the text, you should quickly examine these materials and use the clues they provide to further develop the expectations that you will carry into the reading phase of SRSR.

4 Reading discussion questions at the end of the chapter.

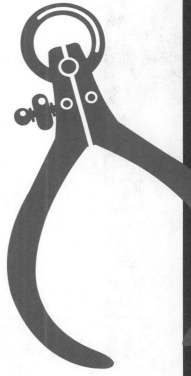

Many authors include discussion questions, test-yourself quizzes, or even writing prompts at the end of their chapters. Reading these questions as part of your survey of the chapter will give you important insights into the passage. This particular surveying step is especially helpful when you are reading for literature survey courses: an editor's questions after a short story or poem can make all the difference in the world to your understanding of the piece, and they should at least create certain expectations about the material that will lead to a much different reading of it.

The four surveying steps should take five to ten minutes for a typical textbook chapter, but the prior knowledge you gain from your survey should enable you to read the material at a higher rate. Also, the knowledge that you carry to the next step should prevent you from having to stop and reread difficult sections in the chapter—saving you even more time.

Let's take a few minutes and apply these surveying steps to a real-world example. Starting on page 50 is a chapter from Thomas Dye's *Power and Society: An Introduction to the Social Sciences*. Take a few minutes to survey the chapter, focusing on some of the elements just mentioned above. The discussion about surveying continues on page 70.

Science and the Scientific Method

A *science* may be broadly defined as any organized *body of knowledge,* or it may be more narrowly defined as a discipline that employs the *scientific method.* If we use the broad definition, we can safely say that all the social sciences are indeed sciences. However, if we narrow our definition to only those disciplines that employ the scientific method, then some questions arise about whether the social sciences are really scientific. In other words, if science is defined as a *method of study,* rather than a *body of knowledge,* then not all studies in the social sciences are truly scientific.

The *scientific method* is a method of explanation that develops and tests theories about how observable facts or events are related. What does this definition really mean? How is this method of study actually applied in the social sciences? To answer these questions, let us examine each aspect of the scientific method separately.

scientific method
a method of explanation that develops and tests theories about how observable facts or events are related

Explaining Relationships

The goal of the scientific method is explanation. When using this method, we seek to answer *why.* Any scientific inquiry must begin by observing and classifying things. Just as biology begins with the careful observation, description, and classification of thousands upon thousands of different forms of life, the social sciences also must begin with the careful observation, description, and classification of various forms of human behavior. But the goal is explanation, not just description. Just as biology seeks to develop theories of evolution and genetics to explain the various forms of life upon the earth, the social sciences seek to develop theories to explain why human beings behave as they do.

To answer the question of *why,* the scientific method searches for *relationships.* All scientific *hypotheses* assert some relationship between observable facts or events. The social sciences seek to find relationships that explain human behavior. The first question is whether two or more events or behaviors are related in any way—that is, do they occur together consistently? The second question is whether either event or behavior *causes* the other. Social scientists first try to learn whether human events have occurred together merely by chance or accident, or whether they occur together so consistently that their relationship cannot be a mere coincidence. A relationship that is not likely to have occurred by chance is said to be *significant.* After observing a significant relationship, social scientists next ask whether there is a *causal relationship* between the phenomena (that is, whether the facts or events occurred together because one is the cause of the other), or whether both phenomena are being caused by some third factor. Box 2-1 explains some of the terms used in scientific study of data.

hypothesis
a tentative statement about a relationship between observable facts or events

significant
not likely to have occurred by chance

Developing and Testing Hypotheses

The scientific method seeks to develop statements (hypotheses) about how events or behaviors might be related and then determine the validity of these statements by careful, systematic, and logical tests. Scientific tests are really exercises in logic.

For example, if we wanted to find out something about the relationship between race and party voting, we might collect and record data from a national sample of black and white voters chosen at random (see the discussion of survey research later in this chapter). If our data showed that *all* blacks voted Democratic and *all* whites Republican, it would be obvious that there was a perfect relationship between race and voting. In contrast, if both blacks and whites voted Republican and Democratic in the *same* proportions, then it would be obvious that there was *no* relationship. But in the social sciences we rarely have such obvious, clear-cut results. Generally our data will show a mixed pattern. For example, in the 1992 presidential election between Democrat Bill Clinton and Republican George Bush, 82 percent of blacks voted Democratic and only 11 percent voted Republican. In that same election, 41 percent of whites voted Republican and only 39 percent voted Democratic. If there had been *no* relationship between race and voting, then blacks and whites would have voted Democratic and Republican in roughly the *same* proportions. But as we have just noted, blacks voted Democratic in far heavier proportions (82 percent) than whites (39 percent). This difference is not likely to have occurred by chance—thus we consider it "significant." The same pattern of heavy Democratic voting among blacks can be observed in other elections (see Table 2-1). So we can make the *inference* that race is related to voting.

However, the existence of a statistically significant relationship does not prove cause and effect. We must employ additional logic to find out which fact or event caused the other, or whether both were caused by a third fact or event. We can eliminate as illogical the possibility that voting Democratic causes one to become black. That leaves us with two possibilities: being black may cause Democratic voting, or being black and voting Democratic may both be caused by some third condition. For example, the real causal relationship may be between low incomes and Democratic voting: low-income groups, which would include many blacks,

inference
a causal statement based on data showing a significant relationship

---

BOX 2-1

The Vocabulary of Social Science

Social science researchers use many special terms in their work, some of which have already been defined. It helps in reading social science research reports to understand the specific meanings given to the following terms:

Theory: A causal explanation of relationship between observable facts or events. A good theory fits the facts, explains why they occur, and allows us to predict future events.

Hypothesis: A tentative statement about a relationship between facts or events. The hypothesis should be derived from the theory and should be testable.

Variable: A characteristic that varies among different individuals or groups.

Independent variable: Whatever is hypothesized to be the cause of something else.

Dependent variable: Whatever is hypothesized to be the effect of something else.

Significant: Not likely to have occurred by chance.

Correlation: Significant relationships found in the data.

Spurious: Describing a relationship among facts or events that is *not* causal, but is a product of the fact that both the independent and dependent variables are being caused by a third factor.

Case study: An in-depth investigation of a particular event. A good case study should suggest theories and hypotheses that can then be used to study other cases.

CASE STUDY

An Experiment in Crime Fighting

Let us consider an example of applying the classic scientific research design to a specific social problem—neighborhood crime. A local government is considering the installation of street lighting in residential neighborhoods to combat crime. The hypothesis is that increased lighting will reduce crime rates. Before spending large sums of money to light up the entire city without knowing whether the plan will work, the city council decides to put the program to a scientific test. The council selects several neighborhoods that have identical characteristics (crime rate, land use, population density, unemployment, population age, income, racial balance, and so forth). Some of the areas are randomly selected for the installation of new street lighting. Crime rates are carefully measured before the installation of streetlights in those neighborhoods that received new lighting and in those neighborhoods that did not receive streetlights (see Figure 2-1). After several months of new lighting, crime rates are again carefully measured in the experimental neighborhoods (which received lights) and the control neighborhoods (which did not). The results are compared. If a significant reduction in crime occurred in the neighborhoods with new lights but did not occur in the neighborhoods without lights, and no other changes can be identified in the neighborhoods that might account for the differences, then the city can have some confidence that lighting reduces crime. An expansion of lighting to the rest of the city would then seem appropriate.

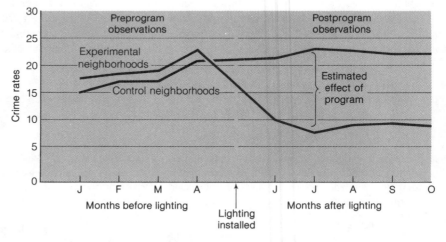

FIGURE 2-1   A scientific research design for crime fighting

tend to identify with the Democratic party. We can test this new hypothesis by looking at the voting behavior of other low-income groups to see if they voted Democratic in the same proportions as did blacks. It turns out that blacks vote more heavily Democratic than white low-income groups, so we can reject the low-income explanation. We may therefore infer that race is independently related to voting

TABLE 2-1   Voting by Race in Presidential Elections, 1968–1992

Testing the hypothesis: Blacks tend to vote Democratic

Election year	Candidates	All	Whites	Blacks
1992	Republican Bush	38	41	11
	Democrat Clinton	43	39	82
	Independent Perot	19	20	7
1988	Republican Bush	54	60	11
	Democrat Dukakis	46	40	89
1984	Republican Reagan	59[a]	66	9
	Democrat Mondale	41	34	90
1980	Republican Reagan	51	56	10
	Democrat Carter	41	36	86
	Independent Anderson	7	7	2
1976	Republican Ford	48	52	15
	Democrat Carter	50	46	85
1972	Republican Nixon	62	68	13
	Democrat McGovern	38	32	87
1968	Republican Nixon	44	47	12
	Democrat Humphrey	43	38	85
	Independent Wallace	13	15	3

[a]Figures are percentages of the vote won by each candidate. Percentages in each election may not add up to 100 because of voting for minor-party candidates.

Source: Data from the *Gallup Opinion Index* (December 1984), the *New York Times* (November 10, 1988), and the *New York Times* (November 5, 1992).

Computerized telephone opinion surveys collect and record social science data.
Source: Lara Hartley

behavior. But there are many other possible alternatives to our explanation of the relationship between race and voting behavior. Social scientists must test as many alternative explanations as possible before asserting a causal relationship.

Every time we can reject an alternative explanation for the relationship we have observed, we increase our confidence that the relationship (as between race and voting behavior) is a causal one. Of course, in the areas of interest to social scientists someone can always think of new alternative explanations, so it is generally impossible to establish for certain that a causal relationship exists. Some social scientists react to the difficulties of proving "cause" by refusing to say that the relationships they find are anything more than *correlations,* or simply statistical relationships. The decision whether or not to call a relationship "causal" is difficult. Statistical techniques cannot guarantee that a relationship is causal; social scientists must be prepared to deal with probabilities rather than absolutes.

correlations
significant relationships that may or may not be causal

Dealing with Observable Phenomena

The scientific method deals only with observable—empirical—facts and events. In other words, the scientific method deals with what *is,* rather than what *should be.* It cannot test the validity of values, norms, or feelings, except insofar as it can test for their existence in a society, group, or individual. For example, the scientific method can be employed to determine whether voting behavior is related to race, but it cannot determine whether voting behavior *should be* related to race. The latter question is a *normative* one (dealing with "ought" and "should"), rather than an empirical one (dealing with "is"). The scientific method is *descriptive* and *explanatory,* but not *normative.* The social sciences can explain many aspects of human behavior but cannot tell human beings how they ought to behave. For guidance in values and norms—for prescriptions about how people should live—we must turn to ethics, religion, or philosophy.

empirical
referring to observable facts and events; what is

normative
referring to values or norms; what should be

Developing Theory

The scientific method strives to develop a systematic body of theory. Science is more than crude empiricism—the listing of facts without any statement of relationships among them. Of course, especially in the early stages of a science, research may consist largely of collecting data; but the ultimate goal of the scientific method is to develop verifiable statements about relationships among facts and events. It is the task of social scientists to find patterns and regularities in human behavior, just as it is the task of physicists and chemists to find patterns and regularities in the behavior of matter and energy. The social scientist's use of the scientific method, then, assumes that human behavior is not random, but rather that it is regular and predictable.

Theories are developed at different *levels of generality.* Theories with low levels of generality explain only a small or narrow range of behaviors. For example, the statement that blacks tend to vote Democratic is a fairly low-level generality about political behavior. Theories with higher levels of generality explain a greater or wider range of behavior. For example, the statement that racial differences cause political conflict has a higher level of generality. Strictly speaking, *a theory is a*

theories
explanations of facts or events

set of interrelated concepts at a fairly high level of generality. Some social scientists concentrate on theory building rather than on empirical research; they try to develop sweeping social theories to explain all, or a large part, of human behavior. Still other social theorists provide insights, hunches, or vague notions that suggest possible explanations of human behavior, thus developing new hypotheses for empirical research.

Maintaining a Scientific Attitude

Perhaps more than anything else, *the scientific method is an attitude of doubt or skepticism.* It is an insistence on careful collection of data and systematic testing of ideas; a commitment to keep bias out of one's work, to collect and record all relevant facts, and to interpret them rationally regardless of one's feelings. For the social scientist, it is the determination to test explanations of human behavior by careful observations of real-world experiences. It is a recognition that any explanation is tentative and may be modified or disproved by careful investigation. Even the scientific theories that constitute the core knowledge in any discipline are not regarded as absolutes by the true social scientist; rather, they are regarded as probabilities or generalizations developed from what is known so far.

scientific attitude
doubt or skepticism about theories until they have been scientifically tested

Why the Social Sciences Aren't Always "Scientific"

Not all the knowledge in social science is derived scientifically. A great deal of knowledge about human behavior comes to us through insight, intuition, random observation, folklore, and common sense rather than through careful scientific investigation. The scientific method we have just described was devised in the physical and biological sciences. There are many difficulties in applying this method to the study of individuals, groups, economies, classes, governments, nations, or whole societies. Let us examine some of the obstacles to the development of truly *scientific* social sciences.

Personal Bias

Social science deals with subjective topics and must rely on interpretation of results. Social scientists are part of what they investigate—they belong to a family, class, political party, interest group, profession, nation; they earn money and consume goods like everybody else. If the topic is an emotional one, the social scientist may find it much harder to suppress personal bias than does the investigator in the physical sciences: it is easier to conduct an unbiased study of migratory birds than of migrant workers.

It is difficult to conduct *value-free research.* Even the selection of a topic reveals the values of the researcher. Researchers study what they think is important in society, and what they think is important is affected by their personal values. If it were only in the selection of the topic that researchers' values were reflected, there would be no great problem in social science research. But researchers' values are also frequently reflected in their perceptions of the data, in their statement of the hypoth-

value-free research
scientific work unaffected by the values of society or the scientist

value intrusion
values may affect selection of topic for research

perceptions of the data

formulation of hypotheses

construction of tests

interpretation of findings

eses, in their design of the test for the hypotheses, and in their interpretation of the findings. *Value intrusion* can occur in many stages of the research process, which is why social scientists studying the same problems and using the same methods frequently end up with contradictory results.

Perhaps it is impossible to separate facts and values in social science research. As sociologist Louis Wirth explains:

> Since every assertion of a "fact" about the social world touches the interests of some individual or group, one cannot even call attention to the existence of certain "facts" without raising objections of those whose very raison d'etre in society rests upon a divergent interpretation of the "factual" situation.[1]

Public Attitudes

Another problem in the scientific study of human behavior centers on public attitudes toward social science. Few people would consider arguing with atomic physicists or biochemists about their respective fields, but most people believe they know something about social problems. Many people think they know exactly what should be done about juvenile delinquency, expanding welfare rolls, and race relations. Very often their information is limited, and their view of the problem is simplistic. When a social scientist suggests that a problem is very complex, that it has many causes, and that information on the problem is incomplete, people may believe that the social scientist is simply obscuring matters that seem obvious.

Social science sometimes develops explanations of human behavior that contradict established ideas. Of course, the physical and biological sciences have long faced this same problem: Galileo faced the opposition of the established church when he argued that the earth revolved around the sun, and Darwin's theory of evolution continues to be a public issue. But social science generates even more intense feelings when it deals with poverty, crime, sexual behavior, race relations, and other heated topics.

Limitations and Design of Social Science Research

Another set of problems in social science centers on the limitations and design of social science research. It is not really possible to conduct some forms of controlled experiments on human beings. For example, we cannot deliberately subject people to poverty and deprivation just to see if it makes them violent. Instead, social researchers must find situations of poverty and deprivation in order to make the necessary observations about causes of violence. In a laboratory, we can control all or most of the factors that go into the experimental situation. But in real-world observations, we cannot control factors; this makes it difficult to pinpoint what it is that causes the behavior we are studying. Moreover, even where some experimentation is permitted, human beings frequently modify their behavior simply because they know they are being observed in a social science experiment. This phenomenon, which is known as the *Hawthorne effect,* makes it difficult to determine whether the observed behavior is a product of the stimulus being introduced or merely a product of the experimental situation itself.

Hawthorne effect
people modify their behavior simply because they know they are being observed by social scientists

Complexity of Human Behavior

Perhaps the most serious reservation about social science research is that human behavior is shaped by so many different forces that it resists scientific explanation. A complete understanding of such a complex system as human society is beyond our current capabilities. At present, human behavior can be as well understood through art, literature, and music as through scientific research.

What Is a "Fact"?

In the social sciences very few statements can be made that apply to *every* circumstance. We cannot say, for example, that "all blacks vote Democratic." This is a *universal statement* covering every black person, and universal statements are seldom true in the social sciences. Moreover, it would be difficult to examine the voting behavior of every black person in the past and in the future to prove that the statement is true.

> **universal statement**
> a statement that applies to every circumstance

A more accurate statement might be: "Most blacks vote Democratic." This is a *probabilistic statement* covering "most" blacks, but it does not exclude the possibility that some blacks vote Republican. An even more accurate statement would be that "82 percent of blacks cast their ballots for Democratic candidate Bill Clinton in the 1992 presidential election." This means there was an 82 percent *probability* of a black voter's casting his or her ballot for Democrat Bill Clinton.

> **probabilistic statement**
> a statement that applies to some proportion of circumstances

A probabilistic statement is a fact, just like a universal statement. Students in the physical sciences deal with many universal statements—for example, "Water boils at 100°C." Water always does this. But students of the social sciences must be prepared to deal with probabilistic statements—for example, "Blacks are three times more likely to experience poverty than whites." Social science students must learn to think in probabilities rather than in absolute terms.

Social scientists must also beware of substituting individual cases for statements of probability. They must be careful about reasoning from one or two observed cases. A statement such as "I know a black family that always votes Republican" may be true, but it would be very dangerous to generalize about the voting habits of all black voters on the basis of this one case. We always build tentative generalizations from our own world of experiences. However, as social scientists, we must ensure that our own experiences are typical. We should keep in mind that the "facts" of the social sciences are seldom absolute—they rarely cover the complexity of any aspect of human behavior. So we must be prepared to study probabilities.

The Classic Scientific Research Design

An *experiment* is a scientific test that is controlled by the researcher and designed to observe the effect of a specific program or treatment. The *classic scientific research design* involves the comparison of specific changes in two or more care-

> **experiment**
> a scientific test controlled by the researcher to observe effects of a specific program or treatment

fully selected groups, both of which are identical in every way, except that one has been given the program or treatment under study while the other has not.

This design involves the following:

1. Identification of the goals of the study and the selection of specific hypotheses to be tested.

2. Selection of the groups to be compared—the *experimental group,* which will participate in the program or undergo the treatment being studied, and the *control group,* which is similar to the experimental group in every way except that it will *not* participate in the program or undergo the treatment being studied.

3. Measurement of the characteristics of both the experimental and control groups *before* participation in the experiment.

4. Application of the program or treatment to the experimental group, but not to the control group. (Members of the control group may be given a *placebo*— some activity or program known to have no effect—to make them believe they are participating in the experiment. Indeed, the scientific staff administering the experiment may not know which group is the real experimental group and which group is the control group. When neither the staff nor the group members themselves know who is really receiving the treatment, the experiment is called a *double-blind experiment.*)

5. Measurement of the condition of both the experimental and control groups *after* the program or treatment. If there are measurable differences between the experimental and control groups, the scientist can begin to infer that the program or treatment has a specific effect. If there are *no* measurable differences, then the scientist must accept the *null hypothesis*—the statement that the program or treatment has no effect.

6. Comparison of the preprogram/pretreatment status versus the postprogram/posttreatment status in both groups. This is a check to see if the difference between the experimental and control groups occurred during the experiment. This method, used alone, is sometimes called a "before–after" study.

7. A search for plausible explanations for differences after treatment between the control and experimental groups that might be due to factors other than the treatment itself.

The classic research design is not without its problems. Social scientists must be aware of the more difficult problems in applying this research design to social science research and must be prepared on occasion to change their procedures accordingly. These problems include the following:

1. As noted earlier, members of the experimental group may respond differently to a program if they know it is an experiment. Because of this Hawthorne effect, members of a control group are often told they are participating in an experiment, even though nothing is really being done to the control group.

2. If the experimental group is only one part of a larger city, state, or nation, the response to the experiment may be different from what it would have been had all parts of the city, state, or nation been receiving the program. For example, if only one part of a city receives streetlights, criminals may simply operate as usual (even with the lights), and total crime rates will be unaffected.

control group
a group, identical to the experimental group, that does not undergo treatment; used for comparison

null hypothesis
a statement that the program or treatment has no effect

3. If persons are allowed to *volunteer* for the experiment, then experimental and control groups may not be representative of the population as a whole.

4. In some situations, political pressures may make it impossible to provide one neighborhood or group with certain services while denying these same services to the rest of the city, state, or nation. If everyone *thinks* the program is beneficial before the experiment begins, no one will want to be in the control group.

5. It may be considered morally wrong to provide some groups or persons with services, benefits, or treatment while denying the same to other groups or persons (control groups) who are identical in their needs or problems.

6. Careful research is costly and time-consuming. Public officials often need to make immediate decisions. They cannot spend time or money on research even if they understand the long-term benefits of careful investigation. Too often, politicians must operate on "short-run" rather than "long-run" considerations.

Gathering Social Science Data

How do social scientists go about observing the behaviors of individuals, groups, and societies? There are a variety of methods for gathering data; some fields rely more heavily on one method than on another. The *controlled experiment,* described earlier, is often used in psychology; the *survey* is frequently employed in political science and sociology; *field research,* or participant observation, is a major source of data in anthropology; and *secondary data analysis* is employed in all social sciences.

Survey Research

Most surveys ask questions of a representative sample of the population rather than question the entire population. A selected number of people, the *sample,* are chosen in a way that ensures that they are representative of the whole group of people, the *universe,* about which information is desired. In order to ensure that the sample is representative of the universe, most surveys rely on random selection. *Random sampling* means that each person in the universe has an equal chance of being selected for interviewing. Random sampling improves the likelihood that the responses obtained from the sample would be the same as those obtained from the universe if everyone were questioned. Hypothetically, we must obtain a random sample of American voters by throwing every voter's name in a giant box and blindly picking out 1,000 names to be interviewed. A more common method is to randomly select telephone area codes and then numbers from across the nation.

There is always the chance that the sample selected will *not* be representative of the universe. But survey researchers can estimate this *sampling error* through the mathematics of probability. The sampling error is usually expressed as a range above and below the sample response, within which there is a 95-percent likelihood that the universe response would be found if the entire universe were questioned. For example, if 63 percent of the people questioned (the sample) say they "approve" of the way the president is handling his job, and the sampling error is

universe
the whole group about which information is desired

random sample
each person in the universe has an equal chance of being selected for interviewing

sampling error
the range of responses in which a 95-percent chance exists that the sample reflects the universe

calculated at plus or minus 3 percent, then we can say that there is a 95-percent likelihood that the president's approval rating among the whole population (the universe) stands somewhere between 60 and 66 percent.

Large samples are not really necessary to narrow the sampling error. Large samples are not much more accurate than small samples. A sample of a few thousand—maybe even 1,000—is capable of reflecting the opinions of 1 million or 100 million voters fairly accurately. For example, a random sample of 1,000 voters across the United States can produce a sampling error (plus or minus) of only 3 percent.

survey research problems
unformed opinions
weakly held opinions
changing opinions

When polls go wrong, it is usually because public opinion is unformed, weakly held, or changing rapidly. If public opinion is really unformed on a topic, as may be the case in early presidential preference polls, people may choose a familiar name or a celebrity who is frequently mentioned in the news. Their thoughts about the presidential race are still largely unformed; as the campaign progresses, candidates who were once unknown and rated only a few percentage points in early polls can emerge as front-runners. Weakly held opinions are more likely to change than strongly held opinions. Political commentators sometimes say a particular candidate's support is "soft," meaning that his or her supporters are not very intense in their commitment, and, therefore, the polls could swing quickly away from the candidate. Finally, widely reported news events may change public opinion very rapidly. A survey can only measure opinions at the time it is taken. A few days later public opinion may change, especially if major events are receiving heavy television coverage. Some political pollsters conduct continuous surveys until election night in order to catch last-minute opinion changes.

A common test of the accuracy of survey research is the comparison of the actual vote in presidential elections to the predictions made by the major polls. Discrepancies between the actual and predicted vote percentages are sometimes used as rough measures of the validity of surveys. Most forecasts have been fairly accurate, but the 1980 Carter–Reagan presidential contest was an exception (see Table 2-2). Opinion was extraordinarily volatile during the campaign; the lead changed several times. Last-day media coverage of the one-year anniversary of the Iranian seizure of the U.S. embassy and detention of American personnel reminded people of Carter's weaknesses. Polling conducted on Sunday failed to catch persons who switched to Reagan by Tuesday (election day). It was not a problem of sample size or accuracy, but rather one of rapidly changing voter opinion.

The wording or phrasing of public opinion questions can often determine the outcome of a poll. Indeed, "loaded" or "leading" questions are often asked by unprofessional pollsters simply to produce results favorable to their side of an argument. They are hoping to inspire a "bandwagon effect," convincing people that most of the nation favors or opposes a particular candidate or viewpoint and therefore they should as well. Ideally, questions should be clear and precise, easily understood by the respondents, and as neutral and unbiased as possible. But because all questions have a potential bias, it is usually better to examine changes over time in responses to identically worded questions. (The case study on "Explaining Presidential Approval Ratings" examines responses to the same presidential popularity question asked over a period of over twenty-five years.)

TABLE 2-2   Forecasting Errors by Major Polls in Presidential Elections

	Predicted vote for winner (%)	*Actual vote for winner (%)*	*Error*
1992	Clinton	Clinton	1.0
USA Today/CNN	44.0	43.0	1.0
Gallup	44.0	43.0	1.0
1988	Bush	Bush	
USA Today/CNN	55.0	54.0	1.0
CBS/N.Y. Times	53.0	54.0	1.0
1984	Reagan	Reagan	
Gallup	59.3	59.0	0.3
CBS/N.Y. Times	60.9	59.0	1.9
ABC/Washington Post	59.3	59.0	0.3
1980	Reagan	Reagan	
Gallup	47.0	51.7	4.7
CBS/N.Y. Times	38.9	51.7	12.8
NBC/AP	48.0	51.7	3.7
1976	Carter	Carter	
Gallup	48.0	50.0	2.0
Roper	51.0	50.0	1.0
NBC	49.0	50.0	1.0

Even the most scientific surveys are not error-free, however. We have already noted that weakly held opinions can change rapidly. Some surveys ask questions about topics that most people had never considered before being interviewed. Then the pollsters report responses as "public opinion," when, in fact, very few people really had any opinion on the topic at all. Many respondents do not like to admit they do not know anything about the topic, so they give a meaningless response. Many respondents give "good citizen" responses, whether the responses are truthful or not. For example, people do not like to admit that they do not vote or that they do not care about politics. Surveys regularly report higher percentages of people *saying* they voted in an election than the *actual* number of ballots cast would indicate. Many people give socially respectable answers, even to an anonymous interviewer, rather than answers that suggest prejudice, hatred, or ignorance.

Field Research

Fieldwork is the cornerstone of modern anthropology. Many sociologists and political scientists also obtain their information through fieldwork. These social scientists study by direct, personal observation of people, events, and societies. *Field research* is essentially going where the action is, watching closely, and taking notes.

Fieldwork is usually less structured than either experimental or survey research. The scientist is not able to control many variables, as in experimental research. Nor

field research
directly observing social behavior

CASE STUDY

Explaining
Presidential
Approval
Ratings

President watching is a favorite pastime among political scientists. Regular surveys of the American people ask the question: "Do you approve or disapprove of the way _____ is handling his job as president?" By asking this same question over time about presidents, political scientists can monitor the ups and downs of presidential popularity. Then they can attempt to explain presidential popularity by examining events that correspond to changes in presidential approval ratings.

One hypothesis that helps explain presidential approval ratings centers on the election cycle. The hypothesis is that presidential popularity is highest immediately after election or reelection, but it steadily erodes over time. Note that this hypothesis tends to be supported by the survey data in Figure 2-2. This simple graph shows, over time, the percentage of survey respondents who say they approve of the way the president is handling his job. Election dates are shown on the graph to correspond to high approval ratings for the winner. Presidents and their advisers generally know about this "honeymoon" period hypothesis and try to use it to their advantage by pushing hard for their policies in Congress early in the term.

Another hypothesis centers on the president's responsibility for national and international events. The hypothesis is that presidential popularity falls when national or international events threaten the nation's well-being. The Vietnam War eroded President Johnson's initial high approval ratings. American ground combat troops were sent to Vietnam in early 1965, but by 1968 the war appeared "unwinnable." President Nixon began the withdrawal of U.S. troops from Vietnam, but casualties continued and his popularity also eroded. Nixon's highest ratings came in early 1973 when the Paris Peace Accords were signed, ending U.S. involvement in Vietnam. However, Nixon's popularity was short-lived, as the Watergate scandal unfolded. Nixon's low approval ratings in early 1974 contributed to his decision to resign. President Carter's ratings were adversely affected by Iran's seizure of U.S. embassy personnel in 1979; he experienced a brief upturn when the Soviet Union invaded Afghanistan, but his generally low ratings contributed to his election defeat in 1980. President Reagan suffered through the recession in 1982, but he was a very popular president until 1987, when details of the arms-for-hostages negotiations with Iran and the diversion of profits to the Contras were revealed. Yet Reagan recovered from the Iran-Contra affair and left office with the highest approval rating of any president at the end of his term.

George Bush's highest ratings have occurred during international crises. He won high approval ratings following the U.S. invasion of Panama in December 1989, and his ratings also rose following the Iraqi invasion of Kuwait and his decision to sponsor a UN embargo against Saddam Hussein's aggression. But his popularity quickly declined thereafter with the onset of an economic recession at home. Bush's highest ratings—the highest approval ratings ever accorded a modern president—came with the decisive U.S. military victory against Iraq in the Persian Gulf War.

(continued)

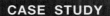

CASE STUDY

(continued)

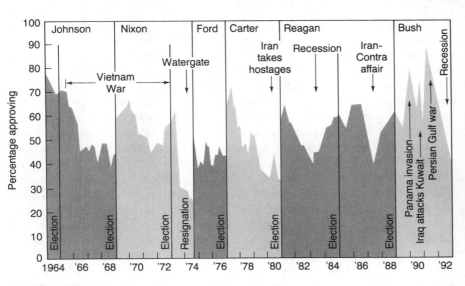

FIGURE 2-2   Presidential approval survey

is the scientist able to know whether the peoples or societies being studied are truly representative of all other peoples or societies, as in survey research. However, careful field reports can provide qualitative information that is often missing from experimental and survey research. Researchers can report on emotions, feelings, and beliefs that underlie people's behavioral responses. Researchers can also report on attitudes, myths, symbols, and interpersonal relationships that could not be detected by other research methods. Most important, they can observe individuals, groups, and societies as they live in their subjects' environment.

Fieldwork research often involves *participant-observation,* where the researcher both observes and participates in the society being studied. Direct participation (moving to Appalachia and getting a job as a coal miner) can provide insights that would otherwise escape a researcher. However, personal participation can also interfere with the detachment required for scientific inquiry. There is also the question of whether the scientist should identify himself or herself as a researcher, which could change the behavior of the people being studied, or conceal his or her identity, which could encourage people to act naturally but raises ethical questions. Some behavior simply cannot be observed if social scientists are identified as researchers. Consider the dilemma of the sociologist who wanted to study homosexual behavior in public toilets. It was not really feasible for him to go on field trips to public toilets identifying himself as a sociologist, asking people if they were homosexuals seeking contacts, and, if so, could he watch. So instead he began vis-

participant-observation
researchers both observe and participate in the behavior being studied

iting public toilets where he suspected homosexual activity was taking place and volunteering to act as a "lookout" for those engaging in the action. He discovered that a lookout was an acceptable, even important, position, and he took advantage of it to study homosexual behavior. Later, after the publication of his study, he came under attack by homosexuals and others for deceiving his subjects.[2]

Anthropology relies heavily on field research. To describe cultures accurately, many anthropologists chose to live among the people they were studying, directly observing and participating in their lives. Many early anthropological studies were intuitive: they produced in-depth, firsthand, long-term observations of societies, but these observations were not very systematic. Some would focus on child rearing, or religion, or art, or language, or particularly strange or bizarre practices. Later, anthropological fieldwork became more disciplined, and anthropologists began systematic comparisons of cultures.

ethnography
systematic description of a society's customary behaviors, beliefs, and attitudes

Ethnography is the systematic description of a society's customary behaviors, beliefs, and attitudes. Ethnographic studies are usually produced by anthropologists who have spent some time living with, interviewing, and observing the people. Anthropologists in the field can test hypotheses by directly asking and observing the people and learning about the context of their behavior and beliefs. For example, an anthropologist in the field may think the society he or she is studying practices polygamy (one man marries more than one woman simultaneously) because it has more women than men. But as ethnographic studies are gradually acquired for a larger number of different cultures, anthropologists can begin to test hypotheses by cross-cultural comparisons. They may find reports of some societies that practice polygamy even though the number of men and women is equal. This finding would cast doubt on the hypothesis that polygamy is caused by gender-ratio imbalances.

case study
in-depth investigation of a particular event in order to understand it as fully as possible

A *case study* is an in-depth investigation of a particular event in order to understand it as fully as possible. A case study may involve an examination of a single governmental decision, or a single business firm, or a single town, or a single society. A hypothesis may be tested in a case study, but researchers know that a single case is not sufficient to make generalizations about other cases. A single case study is more useful for generating hypotheses to be explored later in comparative studies involving larger numbers of cases. However, some case studies involve limited comparisons, as when two, three, or four cases are studied simultaneously.

Secondary Source Data

Social scientists do not always collect their own data, that is, primary source data. Often, social scientists rely on data collected by government agencies, other organizations, or other researchers (see Box 2-2 for international sources); these data are known as secondary source data. One of the most important sources of data for social scientists is the U.S. Census Bureau, which not only provides the decennial census data on the population of the United States, but also regularly collects and publishes data on governments, housing, manufacturing, and so on. Each year, the Census Bureau also publishes the *Statistical Abstract of the United States,* which summarizes facts about birthrates and death rates, education, income, health, welfare, housing, election outcomes, government taxing and spending, crime, national

BOX 2-2

Cross-National Perspectives

Social scientists are also obliged to rely on governments and international organizations, notably the United Nations, for information on nations. This is particularly true when comparative data on a number of nations are desired. The U.S. Bureau of the Census prepares a *World Population Profile* annually, and the United Nations Educational, Scientific, and Cultural Organization (UNESCO) prepares a *Statistical Yearbook*. Table 2-3 is drawn from these sources. The population of the world was estimated to be over 5 billion in 1990—5,332,824,000. Only 250 million people, or about 5 percent of the world's population, live in the United States. Well over 1 billion people, or about 21 percent of the world's population, live in China.

However, there are many problems in cross-national comparisons. Many of the less developed nations do not possess the technical capabilities to collect and report data on their people. Even their population figures are only estimates, because not all nations can afford a regular, careful, and accurate census of their populations. Moreover, definitions of data and methods of collection differ around the world, rendering direct comparisons among nations difficult. The United Nations sometimes adjusts figures reported by some nations to make them more comparable with figures from other countries. Finally, some governments occasionally hide or misrepresent data they believe may reflect badly on their system of government.

While remaining aware of these problems, social scientists nonetheless can learn a great deal from comparing data from nations around the world. Even if we are interested primarily in life in the United States, we can obtain a better perspective on ourselves by comparing how others live. And as improved transportation, communication, technology, and trade increasingly bring the peoples of the world together, looking beyond our own borders becomes increasingly important.

TABLE 2-3   The World's Most Populous Nations Ranked by Population Size, 1950–2050

Shifting population size in developed and developing nations is causing dramatic changes in the ranking of countries by population. In 1950 Iran was 28th in size, moved to 21st in 1987, and is projected to be the 10th largest country by 2025. Nigeria and Pakistan, ranked 13th and 14th in 1950, are expected to become the 3rd and 4th largest countries by 2050. As populations in developing countries continue to increase, populations in developed regions have already begun to decline and are projected to continue decreasing. The United Kingdom was 8th in size in 1950, dropped to 16th in 1987, and is projected to be 27th by 2025, and not on the list of top 30 countries by 2050. Similarly, West Germany dropped from 9th position in 1950 to 14th in 1987 and is projected to be 29th by 2025 and not on the list by 2050.

1950	*1987*	*2025*	*2050*
1. China	1. China	1. China	1. India
2. India	2. India	2. India	2. China
3. Soviet Union	3. Soviet Union	3. Commonwealth*	3. Nigeria
4. United States	4. United States	4. Indonesia	4. Pakistan
5. Japan	5. Indonesia	5. Nigeria	5. Commonwealth*
6. Indonesia	6. Brazil	6. United States	6. Brazil
7. Brazil	7. Japan	7. Brazil	7. Indonesia
8. United Kingdom	8. Nigeria	8. Pakistan	8. United States
9. West Germany	9. Bangladesh	9. Bangladesh	9. Bangladesh
10. Italy	10. Pakistan	10. Iran	10. Iran
11. Bangladesh	11. Mexico	11. Ethiopia	11. Ethiopia
12. France	12. Vietnam	12. Mexico	12. Philippines
13. Nigeria	13. Philippines	13. Philippines	13. Mexico

(continued)

BOX 2-2

(continued)

TABLE 2-3 *(continued)*

1950	1987	2025	2050
14. Pakistan	14. West Germany	**14. Vietnam**	**14. Vietnam**
15. Mexico	15. Italy	15. Japan	**15. Kenya**
16. Spain	16. United Kingdom	**16. Egypt**	**16. Zaire**
17. Vietnam	17. France	**17. Turkey**	**17. Egypt**
18. Poland	**18. Thailand**	**18. Zaire**	**18. Tanzania**
19. Egypt	**19. Turkey**	**19. Kenya**	**19. Turkey**
20. Philippines	**20. Egypt**	**20. Thailand**	20. Japan
21. Turkey	**21. Iran**	**21. Tanzania**	**21. Saudi Arabia**
22. South Korea	**22. Ethiopia**	**22. Burma**	**22. Thailand**
23. Ethiopia	**23. South Korea**	**23. South Africa**	**23. Uganda**
24. Thailand	24. Spain	**24. Sudan**	**24. Sudan**
25. Burma	**25. Burma**	**25. South Korea**	**25. Burma**
26. East Germany	26. Poland	26. France	**26. South Africa**
27. Argentina	**27. South Africa**	27. United Kingdom	**27. Syria**
28. Iran	**28. Zaire**	28. Italy	**28. Morocco**
29. Yugoslavia	**29. Argentina**	29. West Germany	**29. Algeria**
30. Romania	**30. Colombia**	**30. Uganda**	**30. Iraq**

Note: Developing countries are shown in **bold.**

*Commonwealth of Independent States: states of the former Soviet Union including Russia, Ukraine, and Bylorusse, minus Latvia, Lithuania, and Estonia.

Source: U.S. Bureau of the Census, *World Population Profile: 1987* (1987).

defense, employment, prices, business, transportation, agriculture, trade, and manufacturing. Footnotes to the data summarized in the *Statistical Abstract* tell where additional data can be found on each topic. (See Box 2-3, "Using the *Statistical Abstract*.")

BOX 2-3

Using the *Statistical Abstract*

The *Statistical Abstract of the United States* is published annually by the U.S. Census Bureau. Statistics in each edition are for the most recent year or period available by October of the preceding year. Each new edition contains nearly 900 tables. Most of the tables are updated versions of tables that appeared in previous editions. The original source of the data is provided in footnotes to each table, and headnote references indicate where historical data on the same topic can be found.

For example, Table 2-4 is a reproduction of Table 283 in the *Statistical Abstract of the United States 1990,* which summarizes U.S. crime rates from 1979 to 1988. The headings along the top of the table are column headings, and the headings at the left are row headings. In this table the column headings indicate the total and type of crime, while the row headings indicate the number of crimes, the percentage of change, and the rate (number

(continued)

BOX 2-3

(continued)

of crimes per 100,000 inhabitants) for the years 1979 through 1988. So, for example, we can see there were 20,700 murders in the United States in 1988 (note that the number of offenses is given in thousands), and we can see that is somewhat *fewer* than the 23,000 murders in 1980. We can also observe that the murder rate per 100,000 inhabitants declined from 10.2 in 1980 to 8.4 in 1986.

It is possible to construct charts of the changes in crime rates from 1978 through 1988 using the data provided in this table. For example, the Census Bureau used these data to construct the two charts in Figure 2-3; one

chart depicts the violent crime rate (violent crimes are defined as murder, forcible rape, robbery, and aggravated assault) and one chart shows the rate for nonviolent crime (larceny, burglary, and motor vehicle theft).

The original source of these data is indicated in the footnote—annual publication by the Federal Bureau of Investigation, *Crime in the United States*. For more detailed data, social scientists would go to a library to find this publication or write to the U.S. Government Printing Office in Washington, D.C., and request a copy.

TABLE 2-4 Crimes and Crime Rates, by Type, 1979–1988

		Violent Crime					Property Crime			
Item and Year	Total	Total	Murder[a]	Forcible rape	Robbery	Aggra- vated assault	Total	Burglary	Larceny/ theft	Motor vehicle theft
Number of offenses (1,000):										
1979	12,250	1,208	21.5	76.4	481	629	11,042	3,328	6,601	1,113
1980	13,408	1,345	23.0	83.0	566	673	12,064	3,795	7,137	1,132
1981	13,424	1,362	22.5	82.5	593	664	12,062	3,780	7,194	1,088
1982	12,974	1,322	21.0	78.8	553	669	11,652	3,447	7,143	1,062
1983	12,109	1,258	19.3	78.9	507	653	10,851	3,130	6,713	1,008
1984	11,882	1,273	18.7	84.2	485	685	10,609	2,984	6,592	1,032
1985	12,431	1,329	19.0	88.7	498	723	11,103	3,073	6,926	1,103
1986	13,212	1,489	20.6	91.5	543	834	11,723	3,241	7,257	1,224
1987	13,509	1,484	20.1	91.1	518	855	12,025	3,236	7,500	1,289
1988	13,923	1,566	20.7	92.5	543	910	12,357	3,218	7,706	1,433
Percent change, number of offenses:										
1979–1988	13.7	29.7	−3.6	21.1	13.0	44.6	11.9	−3.3	16.7	28.8
1984–1988	17.2	23.0	10.6	9.8	12.0	32.8	16.5	7.8	16.9	38.8
1987–1988	3.1	5.5	2.9	1.5	4.9	6.4	2.8	−.6	2.7	11.2
Rate per 100,000 inhabitants:										
1979	5,566	549	9.7	34.7	218	286	5,017	1,512	2,999	506
1980	5,950	597	10.2	36.8	251	299	5,353	1,684	3,167	502
1981	5,858	594	9.8	36.0	259	290	5,264	1,650	3,140	475
1982	5,604	571	9.1	34.0	239	289	5,033	1,489	3,085	459
1983	5,175	538	8.3	33.7	217	279	4,637	1,338	2,869	431
1984	5,031	539	7.9	35.7	205	290	4,492	1,264	2,791	437
1985	5,207	557	7.9	37.1	209	303	4,651	1,287	2,901	462

(continued)

BOX 2-3

(continued)

TABLE 2-4   *(continued)*

		Violent Crime				Property Crime			
Item and Year	*Total*	*Total*	*Murder*[a]	*Forcible rape*	*Robbery*	*Aggra-vated assault*	*Total*	*Burglary*	*Larceny/ theft*	*Motor vehicle theft*
1986	5,480	618	8.6	37.9	225	346	4,863	1,345	3,010	508
1987	5,550	610	8.3	37.4	213	351	4,940	1,330	3,081	529
1988	5,664	637	8.4	37.6	221	370	5,027	1,309	3,135	583
Percent change, rate per 100,000 inhabitants:										
1979–1988	1.8	16.1	−13.4	8.4	1.1	29.4	.2	−13.4	4.5	15.3
1984–1988	12.6	18.2	6.3	5.3	7.5	27.6	11.9	3.6	12.3	33.3
1987–1988	2.1	4.5	1.2	.5	3.9	5.4	1.8	−1.5	1.7	10.1

Note: Data refer to offenses known to the police. Rates are based on the Bureau of the Census estimated resident population as of July 1, except 1980, enumerated as of April 1. Annual totals for years prior to 1984 were adjusted in 1984 and may not be consistent with those in prior editions. See source for details. Minus sign (−) indicates decrease. For definitions of crimes, see text, section 5. See *Historical Statistics, Colonial Times to 1970,* series H 952-961 for related data.

[a]Includes nonnegligent manslaughter.

Source: U.S. Federal Bureau of Investigation, *Crime in the United States,* annual.

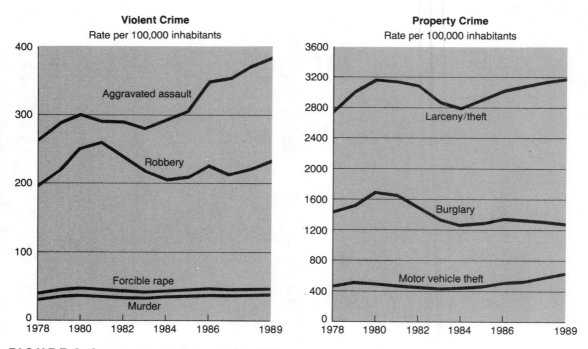

FIGURE 2-3   Selected crime rates, 1978 to 1988
Source: Chart prepared by U.S. Bureau of the Census. For data, see Table 2-4.

Notes

1. Louis Wirth, preface to *Ideology and Utopia: An Introduction to the Sociology of Knowledge,* by Karl Mannheim (New York: Harcourt Brace Jovanovich, 1936), p. vii.
2. Laud Humphreys, *Tearoom Trade: Impersonal Sex in Public Places* (Chicago: Aldine, 1970), cited in *Sociology: An Introduction,* 2nd ed., ed. Earl R. Babbie (Belmont, Calif.: Wadsworth, 1980).

About This Chapter

What is a science, and what is the scientific method? How can the subject matter of the social sciences be studied scientifically? What are the obstacles to the scientific study of human behavior and social relations? How can theories and hypotheses be tested in social science research? How can data be collected? For example, how can a psychologist accurately and objectively measure a person's reaction to authority or a sociologist identify someone's social status? How can a political scientist be sure that a reduction in crime is the result of a government program and not the incidental effect of some other factor? Social scientists are often accused of not being truly scientific. Are they guilty as charged, and if so, why? What are the problems, the promise, and the sometimes paradoxical effects of social science research?

These are the questions that Chapter 2 addressed. Now that you have read it, you should be able to

- define science and describe the scientific method,
- illustrate how social scientists develop and test hypotheses,
- describe the classic research design and discuss some of the problems that social scientists have in applying this design and the scientific method to their research.

Discussion Questions

1. You are about to begin a social science research project, and you want it to be scientific rather than normative. Describe the method you would choose, explaining how it works and what its goals are. Using this method, will you be able to prove cause and effect? Why or why not?

2. Discuss some of the difficulties the social scientist has in applying the scientific method to the study of social problems.

3. Suppose you are a school psychologist who wishes to determine if students learn more when television is used in the classroom than when only conventional teaching methods are used. Construct a classic research design for this purpose. Describe some of the problems you might encounter in applying the design.

You probably noticed that the chapter contains no formal intro-duction laying out objectives for the reader but does conclude with a concise summary, "About This Chapter." That summary poses some important questions that help the reader focus on key issues, and the three bulleted items that follow suggest three main points that the author is attempting to get across. Surveying the size and type style for the headings and subheadings suggests the following main divi-sions: "Science and the Scientific Method," "Why the Social Sciences Aren't Always 'Scientific'," "What is a 'Fact'?," "The Classic Scientific Research Design," and "Gathering Social Science Data." Most of these main sections also have been divided into subsections, reflected in the various subheadings.

A brief survey reveals several other interesting clues. There is a variety of tables and graphs that are used to illustrate various aspects of social science research. Examining these will give you a sense of the type of topics social science research focuses on. Also, most of the key terms from the chapter are pulled out and defined in the margins. Quickly noting these terms will further clarify for you the content of the chapter. Skimming a few sections here and there in the chapter will add to your prior knowledge.

By dedicating five or ten minutes to surveying this chapter, you would be able to draw some valuable infer-ences that will make the three remaining steps in the SRSR process much more powerful. You know that the chapter focuses both on similarities and differences between science and social science. You can assume that the chapter will offer guidelines on how social scientists can conduct their research as "scientifically" as possible and how they draw conclusions from their work. If you are the typical student, you probably had very limited knowledge about these issues before encountering this material, but after a brief survey, you have at least a vague sense of the topic and are in a frame of mind to make the actual reading much more meaningful.

Read

The second step in the SRSR process is nothing particularly new to you. After all, you have been reading textbook assignments all of your academic life.

However, most readers make the actual reading the first step—or perhaps the only step—in the process. Going into the passage "cold," with few, if any, expectations about the chapter's content is a little like walking into uncharted (un*surveyed*!) territory; there is an initial period of uncertainty or disorientation. Mental "paths" often lead to dead ends and force the reader to backtrack and attempt to work through a diffi-cult passage again.

When it follows the survey-ing step, the actual reading is much more productive. The prior knowledge gained through the surveying, though somewhat general and incomplete, sets up certain expectations; you should have a fair sense of where the passage is heading. You will have made certain predictions about the text's main ideas, and reading becomes an effort to confirm, understand, or perhaps correct these predictions, based on the details that lie ahead. Since you are reading to confirm or correct your expectations, your focus is always *forward* in the text.

The actual reading is perhaps the most mentally strenuous of the four steps. You should be realistic about how long your attention span will let you stay focused on the task. In most cases, if a reading assignment will take longer than thirty minutes to complete, you should break it down into several shorter sections. You should also take a short break between the sections and come back to the next section relaxed and ready to concentrate.

Simplify

The next phase of the SRSR process is to take the information on the printed page and simplify it, mainly by shaping or streamlining it in such a way that you reduce it to its key ideas.

If you own your textbook, the best way to simplify the text is to use a highlighter to mark the 10 to 15 percent of the material that reflects the skeleton of the chapter and its most important supporting points. Most students who use a highlighter get carried away, sometimes highlighting half of a page or more. Your objective is to mark only the most important ideas. If you do the job properly, you will be able to review in four to six minutes a chapter that took you forty-five minutes to read, just by going over the high-lighted passages. Highlighting also forces you to *interact* with the material, to make judgments about what is important, what the main ideas are, what support exists for the main ideas, and so on.

You may find it possible to combine the highlighting process with the reading process in step 2. If you can highlight without losing track of the passage's main ideas, then by all means do so.

A second strategy you can use if you are free to mark in your textbook is to jot down notes in the margin of the page. Many textbook companies provide margins that are spacious enough to allow you to write down your ideas, reactions, summary statements, and questions in the margin. In the sample chapter you examined in the surveying exercise, important terms are already set out in the margins, and the margins themselves are spacious enough for brief notes. If you have an instructor whose class discussions are tied very closely to the chapter content, you may discover that you can take the majority of your class notes in the margins of the book itself.

If you are not able to mark in the textbook, you have an alternative. The template section later in this chapter provides you with **Chapter Charts**, special pages that lead you to simplify, summarize, and record the most important details in the chapter.

Read, mark, learn, and inwardly digest.

THE BOOK OF COMMON PRAYER (1548)

Reflect

The last step in the process is to take a few minutes and reflect on what you have read. Your primary objective here is to reinforce the material you have just learned, which is your best hope to retain the material until your next review period. Researchers suggest that more than 40 percent of the new information our brain absorbs will be lost within twenty-four hours if we do not review or reinforce the information.

The best way to reflect on the chapter material is to turn back to the first page and, using the textual clues, highlighted information, or Chapter Charts data, recite aloud the main points of the chapter. To recite, as the term is used here, means to take the information and express it *aloud in your own words*. You are not trying to commit to memory important information word-for-word out of the text; rather, you are taking the information and making it *yours* by expressing it in your own words. It is important that you speak aloud—force yourself to put the information into words, not just abstract silent thoughts. Hearing the words is another way to reinforce information in your brain, since the process uses a different sensory channel. (So far, all the data has been collected *visually*.)

If we could eavesdrop on someone reflecting on the "Social Sciences and the Scientific Method" chapter, we might hear the process starting something like this:

> OK…this chapter is about how social scientists conduct their research. It begins by talking about what "science" is…how scientists use the "scientific method" to try to explain the relationships in what they are able to observe. The scientist works from a hypothesis, which is sort of a tentative belief that is going to be tested. Scientists limit themselves to empirical data, which is basically what can be observed directly through the senses—what we generally refer to as "facts." The chapter also stresses that scientists have to be somewhat skeptical in conducting their research. They can't jump to conclusions based on one or two bits of information. There has to be a definite trend or lots of evidence before they can say that their hypothesis is valid or invalid.
>
> Social scientists need to have many of the same attitudes as researchers in the physical sciences, but there are several reasons why social science research can't be as absolute or conclusive….

The SRSR method can dramatically improve your ability to interpret what you read. It also provides for much better long-term retention of the information. Although your first reaction to the process may be to think that it lengthens or "adds to" the task of reading, it can actually save you time and effort in the long run. Remember that surveying promotes a faster reading speed, as well as making it unlikely that you will have to reread passages. Also, the simplifying and reflecting steps make for more efficient learning and retention. You should be able to review for a test much more quickly and not find yourself having to reread a chapter the night before a major exam.

Next, let's consider another way you might take chapter material and put it in a form that will make understanding it somewhat easier.

On to Chapter Charts

As we stress in a variety of places throughout *Toolkit for College Success*, learners can benefit by taking information and transforming it into another format. Such a practice is often helpful when you take information that is essentially in the abstract world of words and put it in forms that tap into spatial and visual learning "channels." The Chapter Chart is one tool that you can apply to textbook material to simplify or streamline the chapter contents into a relatively concise form that may help you "see" the material at test time.

Templates 3.1 through **3.4** show you how a student might have used a Chapter Chart to "capture" the information in the sample reading chapter in a form that both simplifies it and makes use of the "right-brained" thinking we noted in Chapter 1. Browse through those pages for a few moments, and you will see how such templates can make the reading material much more memorable.

The blank Chapter Charts consist of **Templates 3.5** through **3.8**. **Template 3.5** encourages you to "map" the passage, that is, to use a branching diagram of some sort to reflect the main topic or purpose of the chapter, its main ideas, and perhaps important subpoints. Feel free to use images, colors, or other vivid details to make a memorable map of the chapter material.

Template 3.6 encourages you to list six key summary statements for the chapter material. If you tried to explain to a classmate what main ideas you pulled out of the chapter, you would do so in such summary statements.

Template 3.7 gets you to think about the material the way the teacher might. Some information in the chapter may be very well suited to major essay questions on a test. What might these be? Think like a teacher—if you were making out an essay test on the chapter, what would you ask your students? Write these questions down.

Template 3.8 encourages you to focus on important details. It contains some blocks for you to list details that would almost certainly be important enough to appear in individual multiple-choice, short-answer, true-false, or matching questions. A chapter may conceivably contain dozens of terms, but here you need to make some value judgments. What stands out as the most important bits of information? What will likely make the "cut" and show up on a quiz covering the chapter material? Record in the blocks provided the twelve items most likely to appear on a test. In the space to the right of each block, write a brief description or definition.

Chapter #: **2**

Chapter Title: **Social Sciences and the Scientific Method**

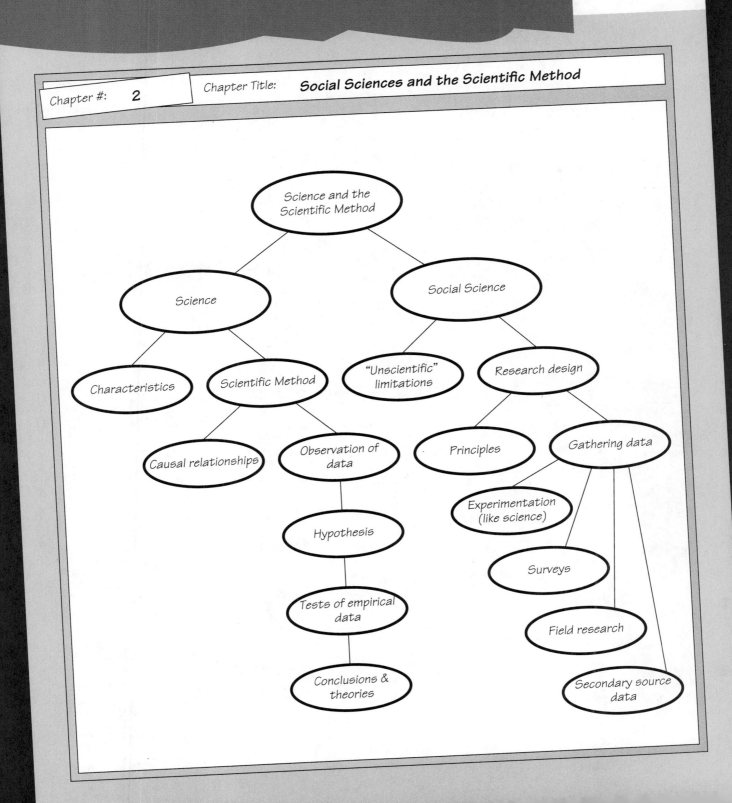

- Science and the Scientific Method
  - Science
    - Characteristics
    - Scientific Method
      - Causal relationships
      - Observation of data
        - Hypothesis
          - Tests of empirical data
            - Conclusions & theories
  - Social Science
    - "Unscientific" limitations
    - Research design
      - Principles
      - Gathering data
        - Experimentation (like science)
        - Surveys
        - Field research
        - Secondary source data

Important Summary Statements

1 Both the "pure" sciences and the social sciences use the scientific method: identifying a trend, establishing a hypothesis, setting up a test or experiment, and drawing conclusions.

2 Science deals with physical data and attempts to establish "truth;" social sciences go beyond physical data and can establish probabilities, at best.

3 A fact is a universal statement that can be verified by physical evidence as true.

4 Social scientists cannot exert the same level of control over their experiments as can the "pure" scientists.

5 Personal biases and the complexity of human nature make it challenging to design research in social sciences that yields firm conclusions.

6 Social scientists gather data by experimentation, surveys, field research, and secondary data analysis.

Anticipating the Test
Most Likely Essay Test Items

Trace the key steps that make up the "scientific method."

In terms of research practices, how are the social sciences different from the "pure" sciences?

Why can't social scientists establish "absolute" conclusions as a result of their research?

What are some important factors that can lead to errors in social science research?

Discuss the four main forms of social science research, in terms of how data can be collected.

The Distinguished Dozen

12 Terms Most Likely to Appear as Objective Test Items

hypothesis	a tentative statement about a relationship between observable facts or events; a belief that a research study attempts to test
inference	an assumption that a causal relationship exists between the data observed
correlation	significant relationships that may or may not be causal
empirical data	data that can be observed directly through the senses
Hawthorne effect	the tendency of people to modify their behavior because they know they are being tested
value intrusion	the personal bias of the researcher, which can taint the study's outcome
significance	a judgment that an observed relationship in the data could not have occurred by chance
control group	a group identical to the group being studied but which does not receive the "treatment" being studied
random sample	a process of selecting subjects for a study in which all members had an equal chance of being selected
case study	an in-depth study of a particular event in order to understand it fully
fact	a valid statement that can be made of events directly observable through the senses
variable	a characteristic that varies among different individuals or groups

TEMPLATE 3.5

Chapter Charts

SEE OTHER SIDE FOR DIRECTIONS

Chapter #:   Chapter Title:

Directions for Template 3.5

1. Write a phrase or expression that labels the topic for the chapter at the top of the page and draw a box or circle around it. (You may, if you prefer, put this box in the center of the page and branch outward from it.)

2. Using both content and typographical clues, determine the chapter's main ideas. Branch off of the chapter topic box and label these main ideas. Draw a box or circle around each main idea.

3. Under each main idea label, branch to at least one more level. Label and box or circle these primary supporting ideas.

4. Avoid making your chapter map overly detailed. If the chapter is especially long or complex, you may wish to construct a chapter map that goes only to the main idea level, and then create an additional map that breaks each main idea down separately.

Important Summary Statements

SEE OTHER SIDE FOR DIRECTIONS

1 _____

2 _____

3 _____

4 _____

5 _____

6 _____

Directions for Template 3.6

Review the chapter briefly and determine what main ideas the author is communicating. Phrase these as complete sentences and write them in the spaces provided.

Anticipating The Test
Most Likely Essay Test Items

SEE OTHER SIDE FOR DIRECTIONS

Directions for Template 3.7

Review the chapter material briefly, identifying topics of sufficient weight and complexity that they may be tested by essay questions. Anticipate what these questions might be and write them down in the blocks provided.

The Distinguished Dozen

12 Terms Most Likely to Appear as Objective Test Items

SEE OTHER SIDE FOR DIRECTIONS

Directions for Template 3.8

Consider the important terminology from the chapter. While the chapter might conceivably have many more than a dozen such terms, make some judgments about the relative importance of the material and select the dozen or so that are almost sure to be on a future objective test. Write each such term in a block to the left of the page and a brief explanation or definition in the larger block to the right.

Notes

Chapter 4

*O*rder and simplification are the first steps toward the mastery of a subject.

THOMAS MANN (1875–1955)

Putting It

Taking Better Notes and

There's not a note of mine that's worth the noting.

BALTHASAR IN *MUCH ADO ABOUT NOTHING*

WILLIAM SHAKESPEARE (1564–1616)

On the Page

Knowing How to Use Them

Taking Notes

If you have a set of class notes from a recent class, look over them for a few minutes. What do they look like? How meaningful will they likely be a week or two from now? How satisfied are you with the results you see on the page?

Many students find taking notes to be one of the most exasperating and difficult tasks they must perform. When they look over their notes, they see snippets of incomplete phrases, sentences left hanging, difficult-to-follow language, and a collection of disjointed thoughts that will have very limited value to them when they try to prepare for a test. For these students, note taking is a frantic, unsatisfying activity.

One of the main reasons why students find note taking so difficult is that they view the task as being similar to taking dictation: they think their role is to listen to the teacher and attempt to write down everything of any value that he or she says. They try to be as literal and as precise as possible in recording the instructor's words, but since most students aren't equipped with the skills or speed of a stenographer, their efforts are doomed to failure.

A New Perspective on Note Taking

Let's rethink the process of note taking. The problem with the "note taking as dictation" model most students have in their heads is that it attempts to make the task a mechanical one dependent on speed and writing stamina more than anything else. Thought barely enters the picture.

Consider for a minute what really happens when a teacher lectures or leads a discussion in class. As we note in greater detail in Chapter 5, a teacher cannot communicate *knowledge* to you directly. What exists in the teacher's mind is a complex mental construction made up of many details in some sort of orderly arrangement. But something this complex cannot simply be transferred from the teacher's brain to yours. What the teacher must do is dismantle this knowledge, breaking it down into a series of symbols: the words, gestures, and other nonverbal clues that are used in communication. These are sent to you one at a time and at a very fast pace—many teachers may talk at 150 to 200 words per minute. As long as you think that your role is to try to capture and record this deluge of individual details, you will find it very difficult to be an effective note taker.

For learning to take place—and for you to record meaningful notes—you must attend to the symbols being sent to you, but instead of trying to record them literally, you must do the opposite of what the teacher is doing: take the individual symbols, construct information and knowledge out of them, and then record the meaningful result in your notes. By "reconstructing" this knowledge and putting it in your own words, you are creating information that is much more concise and useful than what you would get by capturing as many words as possible by the dictation process. Note taking by this more efficient process is much less hectic and results in more meaningful notes.

If it's not working, plug it in.

SEARS REPAIRMAN

There is, however, an exception to this advice. When a teacher provides you with a formal definition or introduces a new term or technical information, you *do* need to record it as accurately as possible. Many teachers will repeat such new information or slow down their pace somewhat so you can capture it in your notes. Fortunately, most teachers depend on textbooks or outside reading assignments to introduce new information. They focus class time on developing a perspective on the information or reinforcing what is important. If you have done the necessary work outside of class, the substance of the class work is not "new" information, so you have the luxury of being a more relaxed, reflective note taker, able to absorb the details and reshape them into a concise form for your notes.

What one has to do usually can be done.

ELEANOR ROOSEVELT

Any new skill takes some practice, and the approach offered in this chapter is no exception. You will at first find it somewhat more difficult to alternate among the roles of listener, thinker, and recorder, but your skills will improve quickly with practice. The latter portion of this chapter shows you a system to help you take effective notes. But let's next turn our attention to some tips that can make almost anyone a better note taker.

Five Tips for Better Note Taking

1 USE A LOOSE-LEAF NOTE-TAKING SYSTEM.

One of the biggest mistakes students make is to use spiral notebooks for their note taking. Although these are plentiful and relatively inexpensive, they have some distinct disadvantages. First, there is no easy way to add the handouts or printed material that most teachers give out over the course of a semester. These items invariably get folded over and stuffed somewhere in the notebook, falling out periodically until they finally get lost. Also, spiral notebooks are typically narrow ruled, resulting in cramped, crowded notes. Finally, and most importantly, it is difficult to get a perspective on your information when you are studying for a major test. You are limited to a one-page "window" of information and spend much of your review time paging back and forth trying to find a particular piece of information.

If you have already examined Chapter 2, you know about the merits of using a loose-leaf system and arranging your important materials in a single binder. Purchase a large, sturdy three-ring binder, and stock it with standard-ruled notebook paper or pages of the type described in the next part of this chapter. Use a hole-punch on important handouts so that you can insert them in your notebook, and buy some pocket dividers to break up the notebook into as many main sections as you have classes. Add a calendar and some of the specialized organizer sheets provided elsewhere in *Toolkit for College Success*, and you'll be in business. You can keep notes for all your classes in a single, all-in-one notebook, which greatly simplifies the task of organizing and carrying around the materials you need.

The main reason you want to use a loose-leaf system is that it makes reviewing for a test much more efficient.

You can clear your desk, remove the pages you need to study, and spread them out in front of you so that you can get a better perspective on the information. As you become familiar with the notes on a particular page, you can move it aside, rearrange the remaining sheets, and continue focusing on what needs more work. This approach is a big improvement over flipping back and forth through the pages in a spiral notebook.

2 WRITE ONLY ON THE FRONT SIDE OF EACH PAGE.

Since the whole idea is to study effectively by removing the pages, spreading them out, and getting a perspective on the entire collection of notes, it would be pointless to write on the back of the pages. If your social conscience tells you that such a practice is wasting paper, you can always recycle the paper at some point in the future when you determine you no longer need the notes.

3 LEAVE PLENTY OF "WHITE SPACE."

As we noted earlier, you don't want your notes to look crowded and cluttered. It's more difficult to find specific details in such notes, which end up looking like a large blob of information. Therefore, leave a generous margin of blank space, perhaps an inch or more, around specific topics or connected details. This practice serves two useful purposes. First, it makes it possible for you to add information later, write key phrases in the margins to help identify the focus of the notes, or pose questions that need answers. As Chapter 5 points out, you will need to review the material several times before you can really claim "ownership" of the information, so the extra white space allows you to add appropriate comments to shape the notes or emphasize important details to make your learning easier.

A second value of leaving white space around topics of information is that it helps visually set off the information into discrete, meaningful groupings. When you look at one of your pages of notes set off by the white space, you will get a sense that there are several distinct units of information on the page, rather than just a collection of assorted details.

4 USE A "CLASSI-FIED AD" STYLE OF NOTE TAKING.
Even when you are taking summary notes in the way described earlier in this chapter, you will still find yourself rushed at times to keep up with the flow of the class discussion or lecture. You can help make the pace less hectic by employing a "classified ad" style of writing. Perhaps you have been amazed at just how much information people can pack into just a few words when they have to pay for each and every word in a classified ad: Suburban 3,2,2. Spanish stucco, shaded lot. Handyman's dream. Asking 75K. **The above short ad translates into this longer version written**

in more standard English:
I want to sell a house with three bedrooms, two bathrooms, and a two-car garage. The house is in the suburbs. It has a Spanish style architecture, and the exterior of the house is covered in stucco. It sits on a shady lot. It needs some repairs, so it's just the house for someone who has good mechanical and repair skills. I'd like $75,000 for it, but I'll consider less. **The classified version makes use of phrases rather than sentences, meaningful abbrevia-**

tions (*3,2,2* and *75K*), and carefully chosen language to communicate more complex meanings (*handyman's dream, asking 75K*). **You can use the same strategy when you take notes, except that since you are going to be the only reader of the notes, you can make the process even more efficient by employing your own individual shorthand style or symbols. Compare the two passages below to see how this style can be applied to note taking. The first represents what the instructor might say as a part of a discussion of the literary term *tragic hero*.**
A "tragic hero" is a common character in literature. Such characters were first introduced by the ancient Greeks and are common elements in the works of Shakespeare and even in many modern plays.

A tragic hero could be defined as a basically honorable and likable character who suffers a dramatic downfall as a result of a significant flaw in his character. It is important that the character be honorable and likable, since there would be little tragedy in seeing the downfall of a despicable, dishonest, or ruthless person. In fact, the downfall of such characters is often satisfying and just. But

when the tragedy occurs to someone we can relate to, like, or respect, then the tragedy is felt that much more deeply by the audience or reader.

It is also important that the downfall result from some flaw within the person himself. The fact that the person has such a flaw serves to make him realistic and believable. If tragedy can occur in this person's life, then we can see that it can occur in ours also. We can therefore learn something from the fall of the tragic hero. Also, the tragedy resulting from the person's flaw can be distinguished from chance tragedy that can occur, such as being struck by lightning or dropping dead of a heart attack. Chance tragedies don't really teach us very much about our character and the result of our actions.

Finally, the downfall of tragic heroes must be significant. For many characters in literature, this downfall includes their death. If you have read any of Shakespeare's tragedies, you know that it is not uncommon for the last few scenes to highlight the violent death of the hero. In other cases, the tragic hero might not be killed, but he may lose his family, some sought-after prize, or self-respect.

93

continues

Some of the better-known tragic heroes in literature include Hamlet, whose flaw was primarily that of indecision; Othello, who was overly jealous; and Macbeth, whose ambition led to his destruction. A more modern tragic hero is Willy Loman in *Death of a Salesman,* whose stubborn refusal to back down from his warped view of the American Dream destroyed him.

Here is how a student might take down this information, using the classified ad writing style:

Tragic hero—common in Lit. From Greeks, Shakespeare & some mod. writers.

Def: "a basically honorable and likable char. who suffers a dramatic downfall as a result of a signif. flaw in char." Downfall by respect. char. = tragedy. Evil person's downfall ≠ tragedy (more like justice).

Flaw must be w/in T.H. not outside or chance circumstances. (e.g. lightning, heart attack) We learn from downfall of T.H.—teaches a lesson.

Downfall must be signif. (death, loss of family, self-respect, etc) Shakes.' plays often ends in T.H. death.

Examples: Hamlet (indecision), Othello (jealousy), Macbeth (ambition), Willy Loman in *D. of a Salesman* (stubborn accept. of warped view of Am. Dream).

If you compare the two passages, you can see that the second preserves just about every significant piece of information from the original. Also, note the use of abbreviations, as well as special symbols (=, ≠). You can use a similar strategy to bring the same sort of verbal economy to your own note taking.

5 USE THE TEACHER'S NONVERBAL CLUES TO HELP YOU FOCUS ON STRUCTURE AND IDEAS HE OR SHE VIEWS AS MOST IMPORTANT.

Students often get so caught up in trying to keep up with the flood of words they are hearing that they overlook important nonverbal clues that could help them digest the information. Teachers who follow notes or an outline for their classes often signal transitions to a new topic simply by pausing briefly and looking at their notes. If you are observant, you can use such clues to help determine the structure of the teacher's presentation. When a teacher spends a great deal of time on one topic, or if tone of voice, more animated gestures, or facial expressions indicate a special interest in a topic, these important messages should lead you to comment in your notes to expect a test item on that material. Being a good note taker requires that you tune in to more than just the words, using clues from the teacher to try to detect both the structure of the lesson and the teacher's degree of interest in the topics being discussed.

Next, let's turn our attention to learning a system of note taking that can result in both better class notes and improved reviewing practices.

I-Notes

The I-Note system helps students gather information and organize it on the page in a form that is useful to them later, when they conduct a review of the material in preparation for a test. A variation of the Cornell method of taking notes, which divides the page into two sections with a vertical line down the page, the I-Note system adds lines at the top and bottom to create four zones. The format gets its name from the three lines that form the capital letter *I*. (You can turn to **Template 4.5** on page 105 if you want to see a blank page set up for I-Notes.)

The zone at the top of the page is the heading area, where you put the source of notes and the date you took them. It is important to do this because you will be removing these pages from your notebook when reviewing them, and the source and date will help you put them back in their correct order.

The vertical line divides the page into two sections. The zone at the left is called the cue column. In this zone, you record key words, phrases, or labels for the information written to the right in the larger zone. Sometimes, your teacher will introduce a new major point with a transition phrase, such as "Now let's talk about some of the arguments used by the Southern states to justify owning slaves." At that point, you would write a cue phrase, such as "arguments given for slavery." You would

then go on to list those reasons in the notes column as they are given by your instructor. At other times, you may not be sure just where your teacher is heading or what the new main point is. In that case, you record the details in the larger column at right, and once you determine what the main idea is, you can go back to the left column and add an appropriate label or term. The main role of the cue column is to provide you with a quick reference to what is on the page so that you can navigate your way quickly through the notes when looking for a specific piece of information. Also, as we will see a bit later, this column plays an important role when you review your notes right before a major exam.

The larger right-hand column on the page is the note zone. This is the area reserved for the actual summary notes you are taking. While listening to your instructor's lecture or discussion, you record in this area the key ideas and enough details to support those ideas. As we noted earlier, you will want to write such notes in a "classified ad" style rather than in full prose paragraph form. When you sense that the topic has changed or shifted, you should skip an inch or so of white space and begin recording these notes.

The final zone, at the bottom of the page, is what makes the I-Note system especially valuable. As we noted in Chapter 1, effective students are able to monitor their own thinking and learning processes, and the comments zone at the bottom of the page helps foster that sort of activity. In the comments zone, you step outside your role as recorder of ideas and make some judgments about what you have recorded. What is the most important information on the page? What is confusing or needs additional information? What do you agree with or disagree with? Based on the clues you are observing from the teacher, what information would most likely be on an upcoming test? What would be a good essay test question? You may not have time to jot down such comments or questions during the actual note-taking session, but as you clean up your notes or conduct your first review, you can spend some time and energy reflecting on the nature of the notes you have recorded.

In **Templates 4.1** through **4.3**, you can see an example of how a student might take notes in the I-Notes format on a teacher's discussion of some of the elements in the play *Death of a Salesman*. Notice how the zones separate the information on the page and also how the notes are recorded in the "classified ad" style described earlier.

I-Notes and Test Preparation

As a means to record class notes, the I-Note system has plenty of merit, but at review time it becomes especially valuable. If you have followed the advice given in other sections of this book, you will have spent some time in short review sessions going over the notes you have taken from a class, but as you begin the final review before a major exam, you will want to approach the task somewhat differently.

You should begin a final review by removing the appropriate pages from your notebook and clearing a space in front of you on a desk or table. Stack the pages in front of you, overlapping each page partially so that the cue column of each is visible but the notes themselves are covered. You will need a blank sheet to cover the notes on the first page. The result is a list of the topics you want to review (Figure 4.1 on page 101). Unlike the page-by-page limitation of notes in a spiral notebook, the I-Notes enable you to get a complete perspective on the information you need to learn.

Next, you begin to recall what you can about the topics, reciting aloud what you know to make the learning as active as possible. When you need to do so, you can lift the page and take a peek at the material written to the right of the cue phrase. You continue in this manner, testing your knowledge of each topic in turn, and putting a check beside each cue when you are satisfied that you can express the information accurately in your own words. When all the cues on a given page of notes have a check beside them, you remove that page from the stack, rearrange the remaining pages, and continue the review until you have learned the last item on the last page.

Writing notes in a spiral notebook makes it hard to conduct an honest review of the material. As you turn each page, all of the information is there in front of you, and it is difficult to tell when you *really* know the material. But with the information hidden and only the topics visible, you can test yourself honestly. What you do not know well will be very obvious to you. Thus, the I-Notes system not only helps you capture the original information into a meaningful form, but also provides you with a means to conduct a review in an efficient way.

I-Note Page

Source:

Date:

Cue words/phrases:	Notes:
Arthur Miller	20th. cent. playwright–Pulitzer Prize winner; husband of M. Monroe; other famous plays: The Crucible (anti-McCarthyism) & All My Sons
Main Theme in Death of a Salesman	Main focus: issue of "American Dream"; Willy's version of AD is warped: success achieved by being "well liked" and knowing right people. W. accepted this view early in life, and has too much pride to admit mistake
Willy Loman	Famous character in Am. lit: "low man" symbolism; perhaps a tragic hero–he brings about his own downfall by flaw in character. Reader feels pity. W. has natural gift for building things, but decided early on to be salesman–was successful, but unrealistic. Pride keeps him from admitting mistakes in life, esp. with Biff. History of past conflicts with B.

Comments:

Need to know about difference between Willy's version of the American Dream and the more accepted version!

I-Note Page

Source:

Date:

Cue words/phrases:	Notes:
Biff	"Golden Boy"–popular, athletic, likable But W's bad example and poor guidance lead to dishonesty. Sensitive: destroyed when he discovers W's affair w/woman: changes his life; turning point in relationship: becomes a failure in life, partially to spite W., partially because of warped values
Bernard	Like Ch., serves as foil to set off Biff: Biff's focus on popularity and being "well liked" contrasts w/Bernard's wimpy image in childhood BUT... Ber. grew up w/Ch's values & at end of play is respons. person & successful lawyer

Comments:

Likely test question ! ! !: "Describe how Charlie and Bernard serve as foil characters for Willy & Biff"

I-Note Page

Source:

Date:

Cue words/phrases:	Notes:
Charlie	Compassionate but "crusty"–used as foil for Willy's character–hardworking, successful–W's only real friend–represents opp. version of Am. Dream
Linda	Dominated by W.–sacrificing, gives W. unconditional love–her attitude contributes to W's failure to accept reality–can be tough with her boys
Happy vs. Biff	Similarities: Both are irresponsible and immature Differences: Happy is more like W. Biff develops integrity (at end of play) Happy accepts W's dream: Biff rejects it

Comments:

Likely essay question: Contrast Happy and Biff

FIGURE 4.1

To conduct a review using I-Notes, stack the pages as shown below, using a blank sheet of paper to cover the top note page.

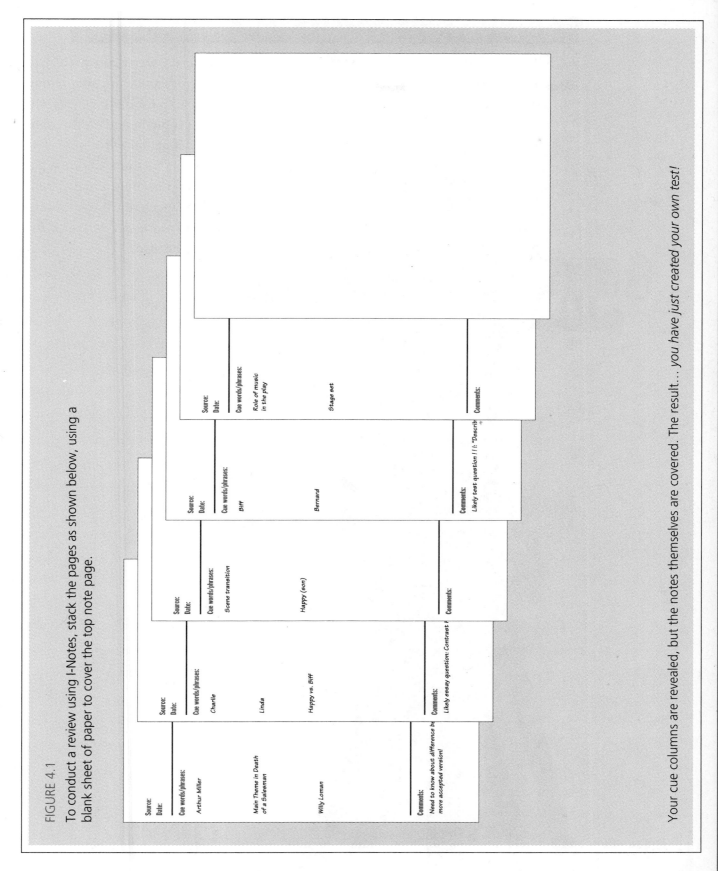

Source:
Date:

Cue words/phrases:

Arthur Miller

Main Theme in Death
of a Salesman

Willy Loman

Comments:

Need to know about difference between
more accepted version!

Source:
Date:

Cue words/phrases:

Charlie

Linda

Happy (son)

Happy vs. Biff

Comments:

Likely essay question: Contrast H

Source:
Date:

Cue words/phrases:

Scene transition

Bernard

Comments:

Likely test question I I I: "Describ

Source:
Date:

Cue words/phrases:

Biff

Stage set:

Comments:

Source:
Date:

Cue words/phrases:

Role of music
in the play

Comments:

Your cue columns are revealed, but the notes themselves are covered. The result… *you have just created your own test!*

I-Note Templates

You can duplicate **Templates 4.4** and **4.5** for note pages. Or, if you wish, you can use a straightedge and draw the four lines you need on your own paper. **Template 4.6** shows you how to adapt the I-Notes system for math classes. On the left side of the page, you write the steps in a math problem, and on the right side of the page, you write down the logic, purpose, or function of the step. The math note forms can lead you to think about what you are doing and avoid approaching a math problem as simply a set of mechanical operations. **Template 4.7** is blank for your use.

I-Note Page

SEE OTHER SIDE FOR DIRECTIONS

Source:

Date:

Cue words/phrases:	Notes:

Comments:

Directions for Template 4.4

1. In the zone at the top of the page, list the source for the notes (class lecture, videotape, etc.) and the day's date.

2. Record the notes themselves in the large column labeled "notes" on the right side of the page. When the topic shifts, move down this column an inch or more to leave white space and begin taking notes on the new topic.

3. If the topic is clearly identified, write a brief descriptive label or phrase in the column labeled "cue words/phrases" immediately to the left of the notes. If the topic is not clearly identified, record notes until you can clearly determine an appropriate label and add it at that point or during your first review of the material.

4. In a review session that you conduct as soon as possible after the notes were taken, but definitely within twenty-four hours, record in the section labeled "comments" at the bottom of the page your reactions to the notes, details that need clarification, likely test questions that could come from the notes, or other comments about the relative significance of the notes on the page.

I-Note Page

SEE OTHER SIDE FOR DIRECTIONS

Source:

Date:

Cue words/phrases:	**Notes:**

Comments:

Directions for Template 4.5

1. In the zone at the top of the page, list the source for the notes (class lecture, videotape, etc.) and the day's date.

2. Record the notes themselves in the large column labeled "notes" on the right side of the page. When the topic shifts, move down this column an inch or more to leave white space and begin taking notes on the new topic.

3. If the topic is clearly identified, write a brief descriptive label or phrase in the column labeled "cue words/phrases" immediately to the left of the notes. If the topic is not clearly identified, record notes until you can clearly determine an appropriate label and add it at that point or during your first review of the material.

4. In a review session that you conduct as soon as possible after the notes were taken, but definitely within twenty-four hours, record in the section labeled "comments" at the bottom of the page your reactions to the notes, details that need clarification, likely test questions that could come from the notes, or other comments about the relative significance of the notes on the page.

Math Work Sheet

Problem Column
(Do the problem here, listing the steps or operations one at a time.)

Explanation Column
(Explain the purpose for each step–what the step accomplishes.)

Simplify: $(3 - 4i)(2 + 5i)$

$6+15i - 8i - 20i^2$

$6+7i - 20i^2$

$6 + 7i - 20(-1)$

$\boxed{26 + 7i}$

Use the FOIL method

Combine like terms

Write answer in form of $a + b$:

Solution

Solve: $x^4 + x^2 - 12 = 0$

$(x^2)^2 + (x^2) - 12 = 0$

$u^2 + u - 12 = 0$

$(u-3)(u + 4) = 0$

$u - 3 = 0 \quad u = 4 = 0$

$u = 3 \quad\quad u = -4$

$x^2 = 3 \quad\quad x^2 = -4$

$\sqrt{x^2} = \sqrt{3} \quad \sqrt{x^2} = \sqrt{-4}$

$\boxed{x = \pm\sqrt{3}} \quad \boxed{x = \pm 2i}$

The equation is in quadratic form

Let $x^2 = u$

Solve for u by factoring

Replace u by x^2

Solve for x by taking square roots

Solution

Math Work Sheet

SEE OTHER SIDE FOR DIRECTIONS

Problem Column
(Do the problem here, listing the steps or operations one at a time.)

Explanation Column
(Explain the purpose for each step–what the step accomplishes.)

Directions for Template 4.7

1. In the problem column on the left, list the mathematical operations in the problem one step at a time as your teacher gives them.

2. In the explanation column, briefly state the logic or purpose of each step—what the step accomplishes. Ask your teacher for clarification during the lecture or afterward if you do not understand why the step is being performed.

3. Leave at least an inch of white space between problems if you put more than one on a page.

Notes

Chapter 5

Education is a private matter
between the person and the
world of knowledge and experience,
and has little to do
with school or college.

LILLIAN SMITH (1897–1966)

The first problem for all
of us, men and women,
is not to learn, but
to unlearn.

GLORIA STEINEM (1934–   )

Effective Review and

Processing What You Learn

Memory Management

God doesn't make orange juice; God makes oranges.

JESSE JACKSON (1941–   )

Memory is the treasury of all things and their guardian.

CICERO (106–43 B.C.)

Learning About Learning

The American writer Ambrose Bierce once remarked, "To that small part of ignorance that we arrange and classify we give the name 'knowledge.'" Never is this statement more true than when it is applied to what we know about how our brains learn. Many features of the human brain, arguably nature's most complex construction, remain a mystery to doctors, psychologists, and philosophers alike.

Although we can say very little with precision about learning, the educational community is beginning to change the views it has long held about how learning takes place. Some exciting inferences about learning have been drawn in recent years, based on research into the process, usually in the form of interviews with learners, direct observations of their learning behavior, and close examination of logs students have kept about their learning experiences. As a result, people in education are beginning to reshape their thinking about the learning process. The following beliefs are beginning to translate into different learning and teaching strategies all across American college campuses.

1 Each of us has learning abilities and learning disabilities.

A great deal of attention has recently been focused on the issue of "learning styles." For many years, the educational system has assumed that students learned in basically the same ways: those who failed to learn in the existing system either lacked motivation or the basic level of intelligence required. Today, while not discounting those factors, most educators are awakening to the fact that learning occurs in several different ways. Many students do learn effectively through the

Next, let's turn this theory into some specific tips that can help you take control of the learning process in your college years.

Four Tips to Ease the Learning Process

1 TRANSFORM INFORMATION INTO A DIFFERENT SENSORY CHANNEL.

At this point, you may not be able to say with assurance that you are a "right-brained" or "left-brained" learner. Some researchers argue that those categories are a little too arbitrary and that we never really use just one side or the other. While this issue is controversial, almost all researchers would agree with this statement: the more "channels" of learning we use, the easier and more thoroughly we will develop an understanding of the material. We have five sensory channels to the brain; why use only one when several are available to us?

Much of the information you must process is in a very abstract form, that of either written or spoken words. Words are abstract symbols that do not necessarily trigger the same meanings in two different minds. If you are struggling to learn some particular information, transform it into something you can see, touch, or hear.

Represent what you are trying to recall as a "map," chart, or picture. Use colors or simple sketches to make the image as vivid as possible. If you learn best through touching and manipulating objects, you may be able to construct a simple model to represent what you are trying to learn. Associate a jingle or song that contains a key word to trigger your memory. Read your review notes aloud, pace, or in some other way tie the information to something physical.

2 LOOK FOR THE UNDERLYING STRUCTURE IN WHAT YOU ARE LEARNING.

With the possible exception of some dormitory rooms, humans are compelled to impose order on their universe. We have a strong urge to see things in balanced, symmetrical, orderly ways. Practically every-thing of any complexity in our world has parts linked together according to an underlying structure. From rap songs to symphonies, from a child's Lego castle to a Gothic cathedral, from nursery rhymes to epic poems, structure is all around us.

The same is true in the way teachers and textbook authors arrange their knowledge. If you look beneath the surface details in the material you are learning, you should be able to see an underlying structure or organizational pat-tern. The work of good writers and effective classroom teachers is almost always organized around a fairly obvious pattern or "skeleton" of ideas. Understanding this structure is one of the best ways to retain information and recall it later on. When no clear structure is apparent, or the information you are trying to learn is made up of isolated pieces of information, you may need to create and impose an orderly, logical structure as a way to speed up your comprehension of it.

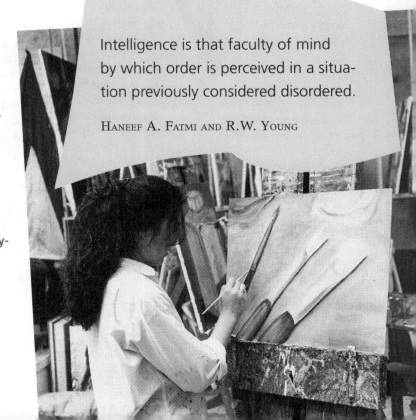

Intelligence is that faculty of mind by which order is perceived in a situation previously considered disordered.

HANEEF A. FATMI AND R.W. YOUNG

3 COLLABORATE! DON'T MAKE ALL OF YOUR LEARNING ACTIVITIES SOLITARY ONES.

Our culture often glorifies the rugged individualist. The person who works in isolation, asks help of no one, and conquers the challenges she faces is deserving of respect. But the same strategy applied to learning can make the process much more difficult and frustrating.

A variety of famous studies over the last several years has confirmed that college students who work together in partnerships or teams usually perform significantly better than those who work in isolation. Apparently, the old adage applies: "Two heads are better than one." When people work together to learn, everyone can benefit from the pooled knowledge. What one person didn't get in his class notes someone else might have gotten. What confuses or frustrates one person may be crystal clear to another study team member.

Two other, more subtle, forces are at work in study groups. First, joining or organizing a group often creates a commitment that members feel obligated to meet. A student who is exhausted after finishing a P.E. class may, if left to his own, simply decide to turn in early and get some rest rather than go over his trig notes. But if he has made a commitment to several other people to be at a study group that evening, he is more likely to put his personal preferences aside and meet with the other group members. Both he and his group benefit as a result.

The second factor may be even more important. Study group work forces the student into an active role. She must communicate what she is learning.

Being a member of a study group gives us a chance to compare what we know with what others know. We are forced to deal with our understanding, or lack of it, in a direct way. The awareness that we know the material and can demonstrate it through our discussions with others gives us confidence; the inability to do so makes it clear to us where we need to devote more work. Study groups make us confront more directly what we do and do not know.

4 USE RECITATION TO FINISH THE PROCESS OF "CONSTRUCTING" THE KNOWLEDGE.

One could argue that the mass of information we have collected, sorted, and stored in our brain cannot become knowledge until we are forced to communicate about it. No matter how intense and thorough our studying may have been, as long as the information exists as abstract, unconnected details bouncing around in our brain, the learning cycle is not complete. Only through translating the abstractions into language and actively expressing what we know are we able to complete the process and lay claim to it as knowledge. Recitation is a process discussed in a couple of other sections of this book. Briefly, it is the process of taking the information you have and expressing it aloud in your own words.

Recitation forces you to take the abstractions, select words to express them, and put them together to "build" an expression of knowledge. Some students may find it more helpful to write rather than speak these words. Whichever strategy you use, recitation is a powerful technique that can help you confirm that you possess true, *usable* knowledge on the subject.

Memory Boxes

What are some of the memories in your head? What is the very earliest recollection you have? How old were you? Why do you think you remembered this event? What did your first-grade classroom look like? Could you draw a sketch of that room's layout?

Can you recall the smell of freshly baked bread? How about your mother's favorite cologne? How does a dill pickle taste?

Try to complete this jingle: "I'd like to teach the world to sing, _____..." What company promotes its product as "the heartbeat of America"? Can you hum the theme music to the TV show "Dallas"? How about "The Jeffersons"?

Precisely where were you when you heard that the United States had started bombings against Iraq? Where were you when you first heard that space shuttle *Challenger* had blown up?

What is your father's birthday? What are all your teachers' first and last names? Your Social Security number? Your driver's license number?

Answering these questions demonstrates several unique features of your memory. You store a huge amount of detail in your brain, and what you store is affected a great deal by emotional events. You store data that appeals to a variety of senses. You have information in your brain that is completely useless to you. Some things have been repeated so often that you couldn't forget them if you tried. Other things that you probably should be able to recall may be difficult or impossible to dredge up from your memory.

Why we remember some things and apparently forget others, why some information is easy to commit to memory and other pieces so hard—these are issues of importance to college students. Perhaps it will help to realize that the information we come to know and retain over time has to navigate its way through three categories of memory: short-term memory, working memory, and long-term memory. To make this explanation as concrete as possible, think of memory as being divided into three mental "boxes" used to store information.

Short-Term Memory

All information fed to us through our five sensory channels must first pass through this tiny little box we call short-term memory (STM). Some theorists suggest that short-term memory is little more than what we refer to as "attention." At this stage in the process, our senses gather raw data—sights, sounds, smells, and so on—and attach meaning to them. In some cases, this is done very quickly, and the information is sent along to the

The charm, one might say the genius of memory, is that it is choosy, chancy, and temperamental: it rejects the edifying cathedral and indelibly photographs the small boy outside, chewing a hunk of melon in the dust.

ELIZABETH BOWEN

next memory category. When the information is new or foreign to us, we have a more difficult time. Researchers have tested people's ability to hold in short-term memory a series of numbers or nonsense syllables and concluded that the average person can attend to only six or seven distinct, unconnected details at one time. In other words, if someone were to tell you that his phone number was 738-4286, you probably could remember it, but if he added that you should call at 8:15 A.M. on the 17th of the month, you would be in big trouble if you had to depend purely on short-term memory. When all the information collected by our STM is new, we retain it by repeating it over and over in our mind until we have memorized it, or more likely, until we have written it down or stored it in a more permanent fashion. During the repetition of these details, our conscious mind can do little, if anything, else.

Much of the information that passes through our STM is not totally new or isolated, however. Humans are resourceful creatures, and we can process information more quickly through our short-term memory by a process called "chunking." Chunking involves mentally grouping details. For example, if someone told you that his phone number was 738-1492, most people would quickly note that the numbers 1492 take on a singular identity, since they remind us of the year of Columbus's discovery. In this case, chunking lets us consolidate the details from the original seven down to four. (Many companies take advantage of this phenomenon to make it easier for the public to remember their phone numbers: "Call 1-800-NEW-POOL.")

Despite how rapidly we can move data through STM, we will miss much of the sensory information that is "out there" because STM can attend to only a few details at one time. Both the limitations of size and the fact that our short-term memory must be "focused" or directed at a specific set of details means that we are able to take in only a fraction of the sensory data that is available to us at any given moment.

Working Memory

The information from STM is dumped into the next "mental box," known as working memory (WM). The motto "Use it or lose it" applies well to information in the working memory. Working memory can store quite a bit of information, but only temporarily. Some researchers have estimated that more than 40 percent of the new information we receive in working memory will be lost within twenty-four hours if we do nothing with it.

It is difficult to measure the capacity of working memory. We can safely say that it is many times larger than STM and many times smaller than the third category of memory. Think back to a recent day when your entire system felt overloaded. Perhaps over a period of two or three days, you took notes in some lengthy lecture sessions, read a half dozen or so chapter assignments, and went

> *Memory is the art of attention.*
>
> SAMUEL JOHNSON

> A good memory is one trained to forget the trivial.
>
> CLIFTON FADIMAN

to two labs. The result is a huge collection of isolated bits and pieces of information. Perhaps you had the sensation of having your brain absolutely "loaded down" with information. That sensation describes a working memory with information overload. You must *process* the information in some manner to slim it down to more streamlined, usable chunks of information, which can then be passed along to the third memory category.

The processing that takes place in WM can take various forms. We can rehearse the information over and over until, by simple rote processes, it is ready to be absorbed into the next memory category. Some of the information is unnecessary or repetitious, so we allow it to fade from memory. Processing can also include sorting and organizing data in order to make it more meaningful or "streamlined." We can analyze new information and compare or contrast it with other related information that is already stored. We may choose to convert the contents in WM into other sensory forms, perhaps remembering a new acquaintance named Lincoln by seeing in our mind's eye the luxury car or the links of a heavy chain. By a variety of processes, the information is "worked" until it is ready to be stored as *knowledge* in the third category of memory.

For most students, inefficient processing of the information in their working memory is the weak link in the memory chain. Each day, a new load of information is delivered from short-term memory: algebra formulas, a Poe short story, two new chapters from a history text, and so on. A student who has made a habit of putting off review until the evening before a major test will discover that much of the information just isn't there any more. To develop an understanding of it, the student must return to the source, if possible, and basically begin the process again, perhaps rereading a chapter assignment or trying to decipher notes taken several weeks prior.

Students who don't manage their working memory well depend on last-minute cramming. Every nook and cranny of their working memory is crammed full, with no organizing system to make the information easy to find. Furthermore, once the test is taken, the information in working memory will likely be disposed of rather than processed further to be added to their long-term knowledge. One of the most important steps you can take to improve your memory is to commit to process information in WM frequently so that the knowledge can be more permanently stored in long-term memory.

Long-Term Memory

Abruptly, the poker of memory stirs the ashes of recollection and uncovers a forgetten ember, still smoldering down there, still hot, still glowing, still red as red.

WILLIAM MANCHESTER

The fraction of details that we attend to in short-term memory and then process efficiently in working memory reaches a relatively safe haven in our long-term memory (LTM). The term "box" is more difficult to apply to LTM. It may be useful to think of this category of memory as a container like the first two, but much larger. It is perhaps best to think of LTM as the storage site for all the knowledge we have "constructed" as a result of effective mental processing in working memory.

Two features are important to remember about long-term memory. First, as far as we know, it is unlimited in size. We have not yet encountered a person whose LTM is so full of information that it is impossible to learn just one more thing. Secondly, knowledge is stored permanently in LTM. Once we absorb the information as *knowledge*, it becomes a permanent part of us.

There is, of course, a catch. (It did sound too good to be true, didn't it?) Just because information is stored in LTM doesn't mean that we can recall it precisely when we need it. Many of us have had the experience of trying to recall information that is "just on the tip of my tongue." Struggle as we might, we cannot come up with the information, although we can say with some certainty what is *not* the right detail. ("Was his name Jim? No…John? No…," etc.) Hours later, of course, when we are in the middle of something else, the right detail will pop into our head (*"Jack!"*). Long-term memory sometimes has a really lousy sense of timing.

LTM differs from the first two categories of memory in another important way: it stores knowledge in a highly structured, complex network. Some researchers maintain that nothing in LTM is stored in isolation; every piece of knowledge is linked to others. It is this linking process that allows us to search and find details.

It may be helpful to think of your LTM as a vast supermarket. Supermarket items are stored according to a system of some kind. Information that we stored recently or use frequently we can recall in a fraction of a second, just as you can walk into the supermarket you use frequently and make a beeline directly to the milk or bread. Information in our LTM that we use less frequently or that was stored some time ago takes a little longer to recall, just as you may have to get your bearings in the supermarket and try to figure out just where in the store's system the toothpicks would most likely be placed. Sometimes you may have to wander up and down your mental "aisles," but you can rest assured that what you seek is there somewhere.

As manager of your own "superstore" of memory, you are in a position to control the flow of information into your LTM and its placement on the mental "shelves" where it is stored. The key is to use working memory effectively and convert *information* into *knowledge* stored in your LTM. When preparing for a test, rather than struggling with the hodgepodge of detail crammed into working memory, you should be able to find the "department" in LTM in which the information is stored, reviewing the ideas and noting their relationships to one another. Test preparation and learning in general become much more predictable processes.

Four Tips for Managing Your Memory

1 DISTINGUISH MEMORY FROM COMPREHENSION.

Many students don't make a clear distinction between memorization and understanding. They are often concerned with the issue of "right answers" and view most subjects as requiring a great deal of memorization. History, they feel, is all about memorizing names and dates. Algebra requires memorizing formulas, steps in processes, and so on. Although some courses, such as organic chemistry, biology, and foreign languages, may require a fair amount of memory work, most instructors want their students to exhibit comprehension of key ideas rather than rote memorization. It is important to be realistic about just how much memorization is actual-ly required in a given course. Don't consume vast amounts of time and energy trying to commit details to memory, when your immediate and long-term interests would be better served by focusing on *overall comprehension*.

2 COMMIT TO REVIEWING COURSE MATERIAL FREQUENTLY.

As we noted in the preceding section, cramming seldom prepares students well for tests and almost always has only a short-term effect. Remember that new information is mostly in the form of details, which must be transformed into information and then absorbed as knowledge in your long-term memory. Unfortunately, this process cannot be rushed. You should make a point of spending brief periods each class day, perhaps five to ten minutes for each class, reviewing information you have just learned. This first reinforcement of textbook assignments, notes, or other supplemental instruction plays a crucial role in preventing the information from fading from your working memory and begins the processing of the

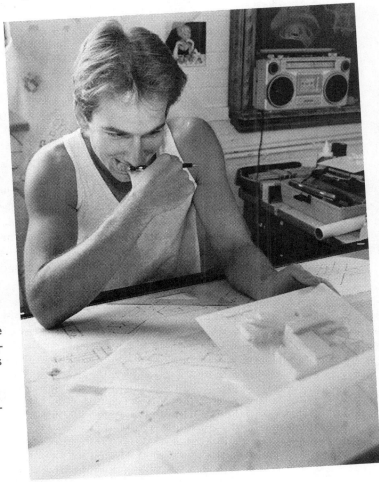

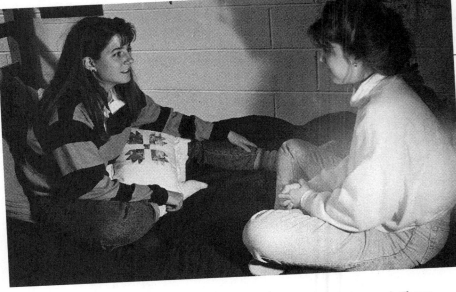

information so it can be absorbed into long-term memory.

You should also plan a longer period, perhaps thirty minutes to an hour each week per course, to draw the information together, organize it, and put it in an overall perspective. You may wish to examine the section on mapping in Chapter 6 for a method to make this strategy especially helpful.

3 AVOID LENGTHY STUDY PERIODS; DIVIDE REVIEW AND STUDY INTO SHORT BLOCKS OF TIME.

Students who plan to study in a lengthy, concentrated block of time are being unrealistic about their ability to stay focused. Mental activity is at its peak at the beginning and again at the end of a block of time. The lengthy middle section is marked by periods of distraction, digression, starts and stops, daydreaming, and other less focused activity. Therefore, only a small portion of any lengthy period is really spent when the mind is alert and "on task." You would be well advised to set aside several distinct *blocks* of time, perhaps twenty to thirty minutes, rather than trying to study for an hour or hour and a half in one sitting. Dividing your time into several blocks means that you will spend a greater percentage of the time in these highly focused beginning and ending periods, resulting in better learning.

4 USE MNEMONIC DEVICES WHEN STRUCTURE OR ORGANIZATION IS DIFFICULT TO DETERMINE.

Mnemonic devices are tools artificially created as a way to learn and trigger the recall of information that otherwise is difficult to link together. Because they are artificial, there is typically no direct link between the mnemonics and what they represent. Nevertheless, mnemonics are particularly useful, especially when they are creative or sometimes even silly.

One common mnemonic device is an acronym. An acronym is a word that is formed from the first letters of the details you are trying to remember. A common example is the word HOMES, an acronym for the five Great Lakes: Huron, Ontario, Michigan, Erie, and Superior.

Beginning music students are familiar with the acronym FACE, which helps them remember the notes represented by the four spaces on the treble clef.

An acrostic is a second common mnemonic. An acrostic is a phrase or sentence in which each word begins with the first letter of the details being learned. Those same beginning music students probably learned "Every Good Boy Does Fine" as a mnemonic for the five notes represented by the lines on the treble clef—EGBDF. "Melissa Very Easily Made Jelly, Selling Ulysses Numerous Pints" works the same way to recall the first letters of the nine planets in order from the sun.

Mnemonics can take a few minutes to create, but they serve as a mental "trigger" to a collection of otherwise unrelated details.

A Final Note

This chapter has focused on some important principles of learning and memory that can help you collect and retain information much more effectively. It is important to remember that the entire process depends on periodic "maintenance." Too many students learn something superficially and then discover just before a test that much of that knowledge has evaporated into thin air. By processing the information you are gathering, shaping that information into knowledge, and reviewing what you have learned on a regular basis, you will find that your learning "sticks" and will serve you well at test time and in future classes.

Chapter 6

Making

The reward of study is understanding.

BABYLONIAN TALMUD (C. 450)

the Grade

Effective Test Preparation

Studie sharpeneth the minde....

JOHN LYLY (1554—1606)

The Cramming Myth

The greatest obstacle to discovering the shape of the earth, its continents, and the ocean was not ignorance but the illusion of knowledge.

DANIEL BOORSTIN

Many students believe that the fabled "all nighter" is the ideal way to prepare for a major exam. The night before a major test, the student gathers piles of notes and books, locks himself in a room with an assortment of junk food and caffeine-laced drinks, and vows to hit the books until dawn, if necessary, to cram all the information into his head by test time. This strategy rarely produces good results if the student has not been spending at least some time in brief review sessions over the material. As noted in Chapter 5, cramming attempts to force a huge amount of information into a fairly limited mental storehouse called working memory. As often as not, a student who crams the night before a test discovers that his mind is a jumble of detail with very little in the way of structure or deeper knowledge needed to perform well on a test. Fatigue and a sense of anxiety about the test often aggravate the student's efforts to recall information.

Another drawback to such a system of test preparation is that what we have crammed in our head is almost always temporary. It is an interesting phenomenon that we often are able to hold information in our memory, programmed to be available for us on test day, but no longer. Just as turning off a computer will erase all the information it has stored in its RAM "working memory," a student who has just finished taking a test can mentally "turn off" her own working memory and effectively erase what had been crammed in. What we learn quickly can just as easily be forgotten. As we noted in Chapter 5, you would be better served by processing information as it comes in and learning it more thoroughly. Spend the day before a major exam reviewing the material, not trying to learn it for the first time. When the test is over, the bulk of the knowledge that has been stored will remain.

Let's next focus on some tips you can follow to improve your test preparation efforts.

Six Tips for Better Test Preparation

1 STUDY YOUR-SELF.
Begin the process of test preparation by taking a good, close look at yourself as a test taker. Do you do better on essay or on objective tests? Are there types of questions that you find especially difficult? How did you do on the last exam from your teacher? Were you especially anxious or nervous during the test? Did you change answers and then miss those items? Were you rushed to finish?

Questions like these can lead you to

Good people are good because they've come to wisdom through failure.
We get very little wisdom from success, you know.

WILLIAM SAROYAN

develop better strategies as a test taker. In the tools section of this chapter, you will learn about ways to analyze tests you have taken to develop a plan for improvement.

2 STUDY YOUR TEACHER.
Few students really take advantage of the opportunity provided them in a test returned by a teacher. In the test is a wealth of information regarding the testing tendencies of the teacher. Although not every test from a teacher will be exactly the same, most teachers are enough creatures of habit for you to predict some likely features on upcoming tests.

You should study the tests returned to you to see where the information you were tested on came from. Teachers may tell you that their tests cover reading assignments and class notes about

equally, but a close analysis of a test might reveal that 80 percent or more of the questions came from one source or the other. This is not to say that teachers are trying to mislead you; in many cases, they are simply not aware themselves of how much emphasis they place on a particular area.

Teachers also might not be aware of other tendencies. Perhaps most of their true-false items are true. Perhaps a teacher unknowingly "stacks" the correct answers in multiple-choice items toward the *c* or *d* choices and only rarely at the first of the list in the *a* choice. As we emphasize in Chapter 7, when taking objective tests you seldom want to consider such quirky tendencies provided that you have any knowledge about the question to help you narrow your choices, but if you don't know the correct answer and are forced to guess, recalling these tendencies can help you stack the deck in your favor.

3 QUIZ THE TEACHER ABOUT THE TEST.

As a student, you have the right to know four basic things about a test: (1) How much does the test count toward your final grade in the class? (2) What main sources of information will the test cover? (3) How much time will you have to take the test? (4) What is the basic format of the test? (Is it objective or essay? If it is a combination, what is the relative weight of each part?)

Most teachers offer this information as a matter of course before the test, but if your instructor has not done so, you have every right to ask for this information. As long as the questions you ask are not jeopardizing the security or validity of the test but are aimed at getting a clear impression of how to prepare for it, most teachers will welcome your inquiry.

4 TRY TO PREDICT LIKELY TEST QUESTIONS.

Try to approach the material you must study as if you are the test *maker* rather than just the test *taker*. Based on what you know about the format of the test, you should be able to look at the material the way the teacher will have to. If the test is predominantly objective, you can look at the material with an eye to finding details suited to a true-false item or perhaps matching items. If the teacher's test is mostly essay, you would look at the same material quite differently. What major topics would best support an essay item worth ten or twenty points? If you took notes according to the method described in Chapter 4, you might anticipate a likely major test question based on the amount of time the teacher spent in covering a topic or because the teacher's nonverbal clues indicated a special interest or enthusiasm for a topic. Research has revealed that students who include in their test preparation efforts an attempt to predict test items will often score a letter grade or more higher than students who never looked at the material from the teacher's perspective.

5 GET YOUR WHOLE BRAIN INVOLVED IN LEARNING.

As we explained in somewhat more detail in Chapter 5, many researchers believe that the left side of the brain tends to specialize in activities that are verbal, logical, and analytical and in details that are arranged in sequential order. When you read a textbook, listen to a teacher's lecture or discussion, and take notes by traditional methods, you are primarily involved in left-brain activities. In fact, most of the learning activities promoted by the educational system emphasize left-brain activities. The right side of the brain, by contrast, tends to process information that is spatial or visual rather than verbal. It stores data holistically, rather than splitting it up into details. The right side of the brain also tends to specialize in creative or emotional processes.

While there is a danger of generalizing too much about the specialization of the two hemispheres of the brain, most researchers would agree on one point: the majority of learners would benefit by finding ways to tap into nontraditional modes of learning involving visual, spatial, tactile, and oral details.

To put it in simpler terms, put some *pizzazz* into your learning. Take those neat left-brain notes, and create a right-brain concept map with details highlighted in vivid colors. Draw simple symbols on your concept map to give you visual details you can recall during a test. (You'll be introduced to concept mapping a little later in this chapter.)

You can also tape one of your review sessions before a major test and listen to the recording while driving to school. Try to translate abstract concepts into models of some kind that you can manipulate—use Tinker Toys or Lego blocks if you like. If you have a lot of terminology to learn, construct some flash cards that you can pull out of your pocket or purse and review when you have a few minutes of slack time. Be creative; try to discover other avenues of learning that might suit your own individual learning style.

> Say not, "When I have leisure I will study"; it may be that thou wilt have no leisure.
>
> RABBI HILLEL

6 MAKE A SERIES OF APPOINTMENTS WITH YOURSELF TO STUDY BEFORE A MAJOR TEST.

We make appointments to get our hair cut, our teeth cleaned, and our car serviced. Why not be just as businesslike about studying for a major exam? Determine when the test is scheduled, and then, covering a span of several days, identify several distinct time slots of no more than an hour each for your study time. Write down these times on your calendar or in your weekly time plan, and treat these appointments just as seriously as you would any other formal appointment you might make. A later section in this chapter offers some additional suggestions on how to prepare for major exams.

Concept Mapping

In the preceding section of this chapter, we noted that students would benefit from translating material from the left-brain form of notes in a standard form into a right-brain image that would appeal to "holistic processing" and visual and spatial imagery. To get a sense of how such a translation might occur, look at the information below:

TEDDY ROOSEVELT'S FIRST-TERM CHALLENGES

Battles with big business

J.P. Morgan—Northern Security Company

Miner's strike

Used a "big stick"

Invoked Sherman Anti-trust

Social and economic reform

Immigrants—widespread poverty

Substandard housing

Worker safety

Meatpacking reform

Election campaign

Opposed by big business

Took message to common man

Called for "equality of stature"

Promoted a square deal

Won a sweeping victory

These notes might have come from a history teacher's lecture on Teddy Roosevelt. The notes are arranged to reflect a hierarchy in some of the sections, with main points and subpoints listed. Though the notes themselves are neat and orderly, they depend entirely on a set of abstract symbols—words—to communicate the message. There is nothing in particular to make the list memorable.

Now look at the concept map in **Figure 6.1**. It has precisely the same ideas on it as the example above, but the arrangement of these ideas is quite different. Some simple sketches have been added: a "big stick," a simple depiction of Roosevelt, a broom, a square deal, and a crude shack. Spend a few minutes examining the concept map.

FIGURE 6.1

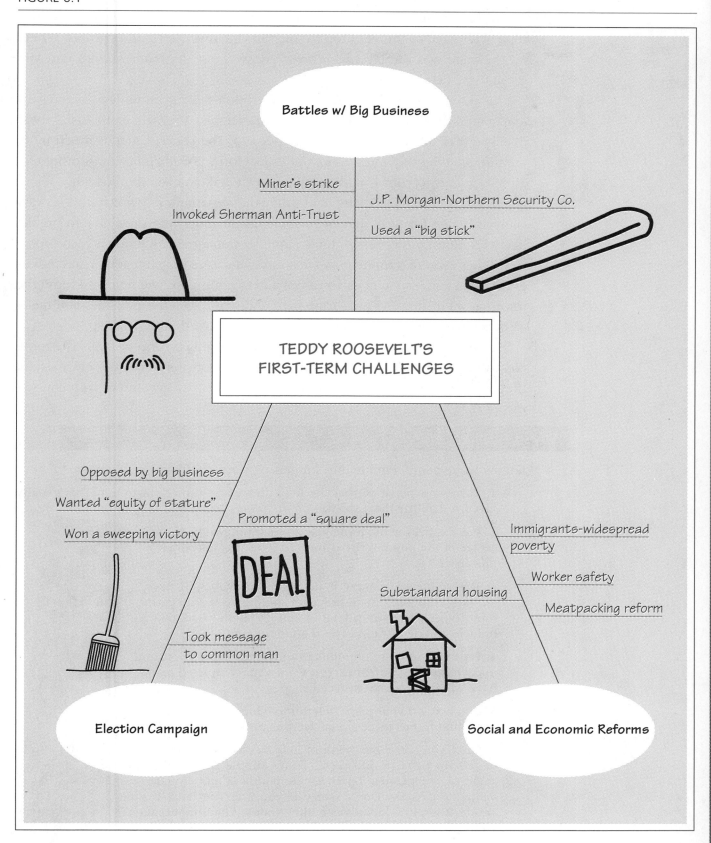

> *A man must see
> before he can say.*
>
> HENRY DAVID THOREAU

Without looking back at the map, you should be able to see in your "mind's eye" some of its features. How many distinct lobes did it have? Which topic was listed at the very top? Which in the lower left-hand corner? Where on the page was the big stick drawn? How about the crude shack? Can you recall these details?

If so, we have just illustrated a powerful fact. Your mind does store visual and spatial details, which act like an extra "hook" allowing us to "fish" these details out of our memory when we need to. The concept map is much more memorable than the notes in the traditional form. By adding color or other creative elements to your concept map, you can make it even more vivid.

Try concept mapping the next time you prepare for a major test. It is especially valuable for tests that have some major essay questions. Try to predict likely test questions on major topics, and develop a concept map on each. Doing so will help you determine how ideas and details are linked together, and whatever spatial and visual images you can add to your maps will help you recall the information during the test. Trust your ability to "see" these images and make associations to help you recall the more abstract words and labels.

There are no hard-and-fast rules for developing a concept map. The more creative and individualized you can make your concept maps, the more useful they will be for you. You can follow the steps below to get started with concept mapping.

Steps in Concept Mapping

Follow these general guidelines for getting started with concept maps:

1. Turn your paper so that the long dimension runs right to left. This usually gives you a little more room.

2. Put a label for the topic you are mapping right in the center of the page. Write it in bold lettering, and draw a box around it.

3. Determine how many main subpoints you will have, and depict these as main branches coming off of the central topic box. The subhead label can go at the end of the branch, and details can branch off of the line.

4. Try to lay out the subpoints in a symmetrical fashion, and make each "lobe" distinct. You want your completed map to have a balanced, easy-to-recall shape.

5. Don't crowd your map. Determine which details you really need, and record these as concisely as possible.

6. Once you complete the branches, use colored highlighters or felt-tip pens to add color. Draw simple symbols beside some of the details. *Try to have several vivid and distinct visual images on the page.* Don't worry if you aren't artistic. If your Teddy Roosevelt looks more like Woody Allen, that makes it all the more memorable!

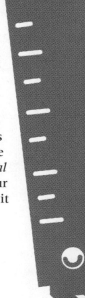

Sifting Through the Rubble

Nobody likes getting back a poor test grade, but the real tragedy is that many students will have similar results on the next test and the one after that. Few students really attempt to analyze what went wrong on a test—whether the problem was poor learning of the material in the first place, inadequate review for the test, or poor test-taking skills. By "sifting through the rubble" of a test on which you performed below your expectations, you can find valuable clues to preventing a similar experience in the future. The three-step process is described below, and **Template 6.1**, which can help you structure your analysis, is on page 139.

> The important thing is to learn a lesson every time you lose.
>
> JOHN McENROE

Step One: Determine the Original Sources of the Questions

You begin the process by determining as best you can the *original* source of each question on the test. For simplicity's sake, you can group the sources into four main categories:

1. text or outside reading assignments
2. class discussions/lectures
3. supplemental sources (videos, handouts, films, and so on)
4. unknown sources

What you are trying to uncover is a distinct pattern. If 90 percent of what the test covered was first introduced in reading assignments, you would obviously need to concentrate more effort on reading the assignments effectively, highlighting efficiently, and emphasizing this material in your review efforts. If a large proportion was not in the textbook but was introduced in class, concentrate your efforts on improving your note taking, and, perhaps, team up with another student to compare your notes and discuss class work with your partner before a test. If you don't have any idea where the questions came from, it's time to assess honestly your attendance or in-class attentiveness. You might want to schedule a conference with your teacher if too many of the questions came from unknown sources.

Step Two: Classify Your Incorrect Objective Questions

The next task before you is to determine why you missed each objective item. For the sake of analysis, let's say there are four main reasons why you might have missed a test item.

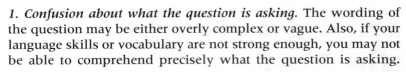

1. Confusion about what the question is asking. The wording of the question may be either overly complex or vague. Also, if your language skills or vocabulary are not strong enough, you may not be able to comprehend precisely what the question is asking.

2. Lack of knowledge. You may have missed a class when the material in question was covered, or perhaps you did a poor job doing a reading assignment or taking notes. You may have known the material at one time, but if you did not review it periodically, it may have faded from working memory. Also, you may have overlooked a major source of information, or simply not devoted the time necessary really to learn the material.

3. Poor test-taking skills. Sometimes you may have missed items because of errors in test taking. You may have lost track of time and had to rush to finish, or perhaps even not finished at all. You also may have skipped an item and failed to return to it, misread the directions to a section, misread the question, or marked the wrong answer by mistake.

4. Testing anxiety. With milder forms of testing anxiety, you simply do not concentrate and miss questions that you could have answered under less stressful circumstances. You may also second-guess your first answer and change it to an incorrect answer because you doubt your own ability. In more severe cases of testing anxiety, you may completely draw a blank or be unable to finish the test.

In this phase of your test analysis, you consider each missed question in turn and make an honest attempt to attribute your error to one of the four reasons.

Step Three: Consider the Essay Questions

If your test had essay items, examine each item in turn to determine whether it meets these basic characteristics:

1. The first sentence clearly indicates which question you are answering. You don't waste time writing the question itself, but you do make sure your phrasing makes it clear which item you are answering.

2. The first sentence gives a concise answer to the question. If you were forced to answer the essay question in a single sentence, this would be that sentence. It should state a clear proposition that the remainder of your essay will develop. It is also desirable to identify your main points in this sentence if you can do so concisely.

3. The main ideas offered in support of the proposition are clearly stated. Your main ideas should be obviously stated, not implied, and they should be clearly marked by transitional words or phrases.

4. Supporting details for the main ideas should make up at least 50 percent of the entire essay. At least half of what you write needs to be in the form of specific support for your main ideas: details, examples, or a line of reasoning that further elaborates upon each main idea.

By analyzing your essays in light of these four basic features, you may see a pattern emerging that you can work to remedy in your next exam. Additional information on how to improve your work on essay exams is offered in Chapter 8.

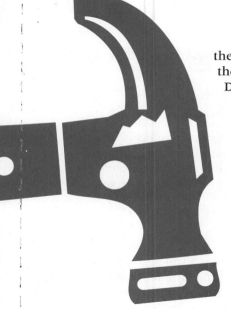

the test. If an answer doesn't quickly come to mind, skip the item and continue answering those that you do know. Don't get bogged down! Using this strategy allows you to keep your confidence level high, and by continuing through the test in a rational frame of mind, you will be making associations with other ideas that just might spark your recall and allow you to return to the skipped items and answer them correctly.

2. *Use breathing exercises.* When you feel yourself getting tense, try to put a quick stop to it by focusing on something internal and separate from the test. The same method has been taught to women giving birth, when concentrating on specific breathing patterns keeps their mind focused in such a way that they can handle their tension and discomfort. An appropriate breathing exercise—one that would not disturb those around you—might be to close your eyes and count ten inhaling and exhaling cycles. Breathe deeply through your nose, and fill your lungs. Hold each breath for a couple of seconds, and then breathe out slowly and easily through your mouth. Focus only on your breathing and the sensation of air moving in and out of your lungs. After completing the tenth cycle, proceed with the test, and try to preserve the same sense of ease you had during the focused breathing.

3. *Try focused muscle relaxation.* Our inner tension almost always translates into tensed muscles, often in our legs, arms, face, and neck. This phenomenon works in reverse as well: relaxed muscles can ease the inner tension. During the test, you can follow this procedure without distracting those around you. You begin by "tuning in" to a specific group of muscles to notice the tension there. Begin with your legs; consciously relax them, stretch them out, and let them go limp. Next, relax your abdominal muscles. Moving up your body, flex your arms and hands, and let them hang loosely at your side for a few seconds. Relax your neck by rolling your head forward until your chin touches your chest. Finish the cycle by dropping your lower jaw and letting your face muscles go limp. With your muscles relaxed in this manner, you will probably feel a dramatic lessening of inner tension. Take a slow, deep breath or two, and continue with the exam.

The key to controlling tension is not to let it get out of hand in the first place. As soon as you feel that nagging sense of doubt and anxiety creeping up on you, use one of the preceding strategies to get it quickly under control.

> *You must do the thing you think you cannot do.*
>
> ELEANOR ROOSEVELT

Preparing for a *Major* Exam

It's "do or die" time. Your government teacher has just announced a mid-semester exam, which counts as 40 percent of your final grade. You have tried to keep up with reading assignments and have reviewed material on a fairly regular basis, but you know this test will be a challenge. You have several days to prepare for the exam. How do you begin? Preparation for a major exam should follow four stages, each with a specific objective:

1 Getting a perspective on the material.

■■■ The first phase of your work should be aimed at getting an overview of what you need to study. Several days before the test is scheduled, clear your desk; pull out your notes, handouts, and textbook, and lay out these materials in front of you. Determine which areas you know best and which might require more intensive review. Try to get a sense of the task ahead of you.

2 Predicting likely test questions.

■■■ Based on what you have been able to determine from the teacher's previous exams and the information you have been given about the format of the test (you did ask, didn't you?), put yourself in your teacher's position and try to determine what information would make good test questions. If the test is predominantly objective, focus on detail. For an essay exam, look for the major topics that have enough depth to support more detailed discussions. Use a highlighter to mark significant details suited to objective items in your textbook and notes. Try to identify about eight or ten likely essay topics, and jot these down.

3 Focusing on detail.

■■■ A couple of days before the exam is scheduled, make several appointments with yourself to focus on detail. Although you may think of detail as especially important for an objective test, realize that essay questions also require detail for support; therefore, you still need to spend some time looking at terminology, examples, and other specifics in your notes and text. Remember that your brain has difficulty absorbing a lot of detail at once, so schedule this phase of your review to occur over several fairly brief, unconnected time periods. Give your brain a chance to let the information sink in—don't try to *cram* it in.

4 Reciting what you know.

■■■ The last phase of your review is aimed at bringing all the details together into meaningful clusters of information. With minimum references to your notes, discuss or explain major topics *aloud* in your own words. If the test is mostly objective, use this time to explain how the details may be linked together. This effort will help you see relationships that can assist your ability to recall information quickly during the test. To prepare for essay items, focus on major topics, and discuss each at length. Construct concept maps or informal outlines on these topics to think through how you would answer a similar essay item on the test. You might want to share this phase of your review with a study partner in the same class. Remember to make your learning and your review as active as possible.

Template 6.2 helps you schedule your efforts to match the flow of the ideal review process from one phase to the next. The template helps you follow the advice given earlier in this chapter: to make formal appointments with yourself to ensure that you allow enough time to prepare for the test and to schedule the review periods in fairly short periods spread out over several days.

Learning without thought is labor lost...

CONFUCIUS

Exam Preparation Sheet

SEE OTHER SIDE FOR DIRECTIONS

PERSPECTIVE APPOINTMENT

Date: _____
Time: _____

QUESTION PREDICTION APPOINTMENT

Date: _____
Time: _____

DETAIL APPOINTMENTS

Date: _____   Date: _____   Date: _____
Time: _____   Time: _____   Time: _____

RECITATION APPOINTMENTS

Date: _____   Date: _____   Date: _____
Time: _____   Time: _____   Time: _____

EXAM!

Directions for Template 6.2

1. Make an appointment with yourself to go over the materials the test is to cover and get a perspective on the task ahead of you. Allow thirty minutes or so for this appointment, and schedule it several days in advance of the test itself. List this appointment on your "Student's Week at a Glance" sheet or similar daily or weekly planner.

2. Make a second appointment with yourself to examine the material the test is to cover and to predict likely test questions. Use comments you may have recorded in your notes to help you identify likely questions. Allow thirty to forty-five minutes for this appointment and schedule it after the preceding block but several days in advance of the test. List this appointment on your "Student's Week at a Glance" sheet or similar daily or weekly planner.

3. Schedule several appointments with yourself to begin to go over the detail that the test is to cover. You may need to schedule only one or two of these if the test is predominantly essay or three or four if it is predominantly objective. Schedule these over a two- or three-day period before the test. Allow thirty minutes or so for each appointment, and again, list these appointments on your "Student's Week at a Glance" sheet or similar daily or weekly planner.

4. Schedule several appointments with yourself to recite what you know about the material. Lay out your notes as described in Chapter 4, and with minimal references to your notes, express aloud and in your own words the knowledge you have on the topics. Allow thirty to forty-five minutes for each such appointment, and schedule them in several blocks of time within the last twenty-four hours before the test. List these appointments on your "Student's Week at a Glance" sheet or similar daily or weekly planner.

Facing Facts

Who understands ill, answers ill.

NATHAN BAILEY (?–1742)

Best on Objective Tests

You can't expect to
hit the jackpot
if you don't put a few nickels
in the machine.

FLIP WILSON (1933–   )

What Is an "Objective" Test?

That's a valid question. What does an instructor mean when she says that your first exam will be an "objective" test? We normally think of the word *objective* as meaning "fair" or "impartial." Does that mean that essay tests, which we refer to as "subjective" exams, are therefore somehow biased or unfair? Given the choice, an objective test sounds like the better alternative. But in truth, objective tests offer the student a unique set of challenges and difficulties.

What we refer to as objective tests are usually some combination of multiple-choice, true-false, or matching formats. The term *objective* is probably not a good label. All tests carry some biases—in the selection of what was asked and what wasn't, in the use of language, and in the determination of what is correct or "true." Rather than referring to these tests as objective, we would be more accurate to call them "discrete" exams, meaning that the acceptable answers to any one item are limited to a number of alternatives: true or false; *a*, *b*, *c*, or *d*. *Within the context of the test*, items are either right or wrong. There is no middle ground.

Such exams are falling out of favor these days on college campuses. They are often criticized for testing "lower-level thinking skills" and for not asking students to communicate in a real world way what they have learned. Although objective exams can be developed to test higher-order thinking skills, such tests are demanding to construct. Instead, many college instructors depend on objective items to test the students' grasp of "factual" knowledge in the course, while employing essay items to measure students' ability to synthesize the information and deal with it on a broader, more abstract level.

To help you do a better job of taking objective tests, let's consider two important background elements: language and logic.

The Role of Language in Objective Tests

We can make several generalizations about the nature of language that can help you approach objective tests more effectively:

1. A concern for accuracy and precision in expression typically results in longer statements.

You may have observed that broad, sweeping generalizations can be expressed quite briefly:

Men are physically stronger than women.

American cars are gas-guzzlers.

Most people would dispute the validity of such statements. We often dis-count generalizations like these simply because they typically reflect per-sonal biases and oversimplify situations that vary a great deal. Some ele-ment of truth may be lurking behind such sweeping statements, but to express ideas more accurately, we must *add language*. Notice how the state-ments on page 150 become increasingly valid with the addition of language that qualifies and clarifies the point being made:

Most men are physically stronger than most women.

Most men have a skeletal frame and muscular structure capable of greater strength than that of most women.

Because of physiological differences and cultural conditioning, the typical male is able to exhibit greater physical strength than the typical female.

Some American cars are gas-guzzlers.

Some American cars, especially older luxury models, are gas-guzzlers.

Some American cars, especially older luxury models, average fewer than sixteen miles per gallon.

The addition of qualifying expressions, such as "most" or "especially older luxury models," and more descriptive verbs, nouns, and modifiers increase the accuracy of the statements.

Accuracy, of course, is a major concern when an instructor creates a test item. Because the correct answer to an objective question is supposed to be unquestionable, no teacher looks forward to arguing the merits of his test when he returns the graded exams to students. *You can therefore assume that "true" items and the correct answers on multiple-choice items will reflect greater con-cern for phrasing and accuracy.*

2. The truth or validity of many objective items centers around the use of either qualifying or absolute terms.

Whether a statement is true or false, or whether the answer on a mul-tiple-choice item is *b* or *c* is often a question of degree that is expressed through either absolute or qualifying language. For example, which of the statements below and on page 152 would you say is most valid?

All labor unions support Democratic presidential candidates.

Labor unions support Democratic presidential candidates.

Almost all labor unions support Democratic presidential candidates.

Most labor unions support Democratic presidential candidates.

Some labor unions support Democratic presidential candidates.

Some labor unions often support Democratic presidential candidates.

The first two statements are absolute statements. The first uses the absolute term *all* to state a universal "truth," whereas the second, by failing to provide qualifiers, implies a universal truth. The remaining statements use qualifying terms to avoid the absoluteness of the first two. You could argue that either the fourth or fifth statement is the most accurate, whereas the last statement contains so many qualifiers that it says very little and is therefore the least arguable of all.

It may help you to think of this issue of degree as a continuum, as shown below:

Positive absolutes	High-degree qualifiers	Low-degree qualifiers	Negative absolutes
always invariably constantly	almost always usually often frequently typically	sometimes occasionally seldom rarely	never
every all	almost all most many a majority	some few a minority	no none

The first row might be called the "continuum of time or frequency." Words along that continuum express how often something occurs or something is true. The second row of words is the "continuum of inclusion." Such words express whether something belongs or may be included within a class or group. Most tests will have objective items whose answers hinge on whether absoluteness or some degree of probability is more accurate.

3. The addition of negative terms will make the item more difficult for most students.

Most students find more difficult items that contain negative words such as *no* and *not*, or negative prefixes such as *un-*, *non-*, *il-*, *dis-*, and *in-*. Such elements can simply be overlooked in a casual reading of a question, but even when students note such words, they sometimes must mentally "turn the statement around" in order to evaluate it. We often have difficulty thinking of things in negative terms. For example, if I ask you whether an accident you had was unavoidable, you probably have difficulty assessing that question unless you turn it around to a positive form: "Could I have avoided the accident?" (Or to use an example taken from a popular commercial, it's hard to imagine what is meant by an "uncola" unless you first consider what a "cola" is.)

When two or more negatives occur in a statement, they often have the strange effect of canceling out each other. What does the following statement really say?

> *It is illogical to assume that President Bush was not "in the loop" on the arms-for-hostages negotiations.*

The following says exactly the same thing:

> *It is logical to assume that President Bush was "in the loop" on the arms-for-hostages negotiations.*

You will want to read such statements very carefully. It is not unlikely that such questions will leave you unenlightened even when they do not contain misinformation!

The Role of Logic in Objective Tests

Your ability to think logically is also an important element in doing well on objective tests. Your understanding of the way the "world works" and your ability to weigh alternatives and possibilities can help you narrow down your choices on objective test items.

For example, we have all seen the multiple-choice items "all of the above" and "none of the above." Let's say you are taking the standard multiple-choice test, that is, a test in which only one choice can be correct. You are considering these four options on a particular test item:

a. **blinkant norbs**
b. **frabent mabits**
c. **megid trids**
d. **all of the above**

If your knowledge of the subject matter tells you that blinkant norbs is a valid answer and that megid trids is also valid, then it doesn't matter whether you know anything at all about frabent mabits. Since only *one answer* can be correct, the correct answer would have to be "all of the above."

Another quick example. Suppose you saw this item on a test:

The probability of the average person being a victim of a crime in any given calendar year is approximately

    a. 10%   **c. 20%**
    b. 15%   **d. 22%**

Even if you knew nothing about what the question is asking, your use of logic could help you improve your odds. First, note that the question contains the word *approximately*. It would not be logical to select 22%, because that number suggests a *precise* answer rather than an approximate one. Moreover, 20% is also not a likely correct answer, since it is close to 22%; in terms of approximations, one could argue that either 20% or 22% could be correct. Thus, a logical choice would be one of the other two numbers, either 10% or 15%.

We carry a variety of other assumptions into exams. One is that because teachers are often creatures of habit, what we learn about testing tendencies from exams given early in the semester can help us in later exams. We can also assume that correct answers on multiple-choice tests will probably not contain grammatical errors or awkward phrasing, but that the decoy items may not have received the same careful scrutiny.

While how well we do on an exam boils down primarily to how much we know about the subject matter, careful analysis of language and the application of logic can help us make judgments about test items that can result in improved performance.

Some Perspectives on Common Formats

Before we begin to examine a specific strategy to use in objective exams, let's first get an overview of the three most common types of objective exams.

Multiple-Choice Questions

Probably the most common of all formats, the multiple-choice exam is the form many students prefer. As a student once remarked, "I know the answer is there somewhere!" Although multiple-choice formats can vary, items typically consist of a stem, a correct answer, and three to four "decoys." The stem can either be a complete sentence (*What is the main impact of increased inflation on the economy?*) or the first part of a sentence that the best answer will complete (*The main impact of increased inflation on the economy is …*) It is important to keep in mind that one of the four or five choices should be thought of as the "best" answer rather than the "correct" answer. It is possible that other answers not included in the choices might also be correct, but you need to consider *only the four or five choices in relation to one another.*

You might find it helpful to use the following strategy when you take multiple-choice exams. First, cover up the choices for an item, read the stem, and see whether the correct answer comes to mind. Then look at the choices and see whether the answer you came up with is listed there. You may find that using this technique helps you avoid confusion and the tendency to second-guess yourself, which can occur if you start by measuring the four or five choices against each other.

> *It isn't so astounding, the number of things I can remember, as the number of things I can remember that aren't so.*
>
> MARK TWAIN

True-False Questions

True-false exams can be a challenge if students don't make a distinction between "absolute truth" and what we might call "rational truth." As most critical thinkers and philosophers know, very few, if any, statements are absolutely true. The world is so varied that we can find exceptions to almost any notion that people hold as "true." What teachers are asking you to judge on true-false tests are rational truths, which are *those statements that are valid within the context of the material covered in the class.* Students who confuse these two types of "truth" have a tendency to read too much into true-false items and go beyond the scope of the course material when answering the questions. In considering a statement like "Dogs are mammalian quadrupeds of the canine family," such a student might think, "Now *quadruped* means 'four-legged,' and my uncle Ned used to have fox terrier that lost his leg in an accident. Therefore, this statement isn't true all of the time, so I'll mark false." Such thinking obviously goes outside the context of the course material and can result in disastrous scores on true-false items.

To judge a statement true, however, you need to establish that it is more than just "mostly true." Any detail within the statement that is definitely inconsistent with course content should lead you to judge the item false. Consider this simple example:

> *In 1492, Christopher Columbus, a Portuguese explorer, discovered North America in his effort to find another trade route to the West Indies.*

Although this statement is "mostly true," Columbus wasn't Portuguese. There is a specific inaccuracy in the sentence, so you're justified in marking the item "false."

True-false items that have more than one part are more complicated. Consider the difference in these two statements:

> *Ronald Reagan brought a renewed sense of optimism to America and won his campaign for the Presidency in 1980.*

> *Ronald Reagan brought a renewed sense of optimism to America and therefore won his campaign for the Presidency.*

The first statement has two parts that you must consider separately in order to determine whether to judge this item true: did Ronald Reagan bring a renewed sense of optimism, and did he win the campaign? The second example is more complicated because of the word *therefore*. Such a transition word suggests that the first statement caused or contributed to the second. Now judging the item true or false is more complicated, because three issues must be considered. You must be aware that such items will demand more of your judgment than statements of a simpler structure.

Matching Questions

Most students have learned the cardinal rule about matching questions: First determine whether the number of items in the left column is equal to the number of items in the right. If they are equal, of course, the student has an advantage. Teachers often "plant" a few extra terms in the right column just to make sure students can't use a process of elimination to guess correct answers to the last couple of items answered.

If you are allowed to mark on the exam, strike out the choices in one column as you make your matches. This not only prevents you from accidentally using one item twice, but also saves time by eliminating distracting choices.

In some matching tests, the left column may be a list of words or brief terms, whereas the right column may consist of longer definitions or explanations. In such a case, you can save time by working from the right column back to the left. Scanning the left column as you look for matches is much quicker than repeatedly scanning the longer entries in the right column.

   With this background information about common formats, let's next consider some "generic" tips you can use no matter what type of objective test you encounter.

Five Tips to Better Objective Test Scores

1 DON'T GET CAUGHT UP IN "MIND GAMES" OR GIMMICKRY.
This chapter offers strategies that can help you improve your test scores, but one point cannot be overstated: *apply such strategies only after you have exhausted your knowledge on the subject.* These tips are no substitute for thorough preparation. Only *after* you have applied all you know to answer the question should you consider how language clues, logic, and past experiences with the teacher's tests can help you increase your odds of making a better guess.

2 MARK—OR AT LEAST NOTE—PIVOTAL LANGUAGE IN TEST ITEMS, ESPECIALLY ABSOLUTE TERMS AND NEGATIVES.
If your instructor lets you mark on your test, make a point of underlining words like *always* or *invariably*, as well as any negative words or prefixes you uncover. Remember that the validity or "truth" of a test item often pivots on such words.

3 PAY ATTENTION TO LAST-MINUTE DIRECTIONS OR ORAL COMMENTS FROM THE INSTRUCTOR.
Instructors sometimes discover problem items after the test is printed. Perhaps other class sections have taken the test and misunderstood what an item asks. Teachers often try to head off problems by commenting on such items or making corrections. At other times, they may want to go over the directions to a section of the test, emphasizing how to approach the section or clarifying the source of some questions. A surprising number of students never hear these comments! Almost any teacher can provide you with anecdotes about students tuning out the teacher once the test is in hand and making serious blunders as a result.

4 GET A MEASURE OF THE TEST AND DETERMINE HOW YOU CAN APPORTION YOUR TIME EFFECTIVELY.
Look over the test, see how much each objective item is worth, and determine roughly how much time and effort you can afford to devote to each. This tip is especially valuable when taking tests consisting of both objective items and essay items. If you have twenty-five objective items worth fifty points and two essay items worth a total of fifty more, you can hurt your overall performance by getting bogged down and wasting time on a couple of objective items worth just two points each. At some point, you need to make your best guess and move on. You can't afford to use up too much time on such items when you know you will need to allow quite a bit of time for the essay questions.

People seldom hit what they do not aim at.

Henry David Thoreau

5 DETERMINE YOUR INSTRUCTOR'S TENDENCIES AND CONSIDER THESE AS YOU WEIGH CHOICES ON OBJECTIVE ITEMS.
As suggested in Chapter 6, every test you get back from a teacher is a valuable source of information that can help you on future exams. Many teachers don't realize that they have testing habits that appear in almost every exam they make out. For one teacher, it may be that 70 percent of the true-false questions have false as the correct answer. Such a teacher

may pride himself on teaching students critical-thinking skills—in particular, how to find flaws in generalizations or common misunderstandings about the subject matter. Another teacher might not be aware that the *a* option is very seldom a correct answer on her multiple-choice items. Perhaps she is unconsciously forcing the students to read all of the options before choosing an answer, and therefore "stacks" the answers in the *c* or *d* options. Other teachers habitually use "all of the above" and "none of the above" as throw-away options just because they are an easy decoy to come up with. Still other instructors might make up "gobbledygook" terms for decoy items on multiple-choice tests or perhaps throw in an absurd option to inject humor into the test. Take such factors into consideration if you are forced to guess on a test item.

Step-by-Step to Better Test Scores

When confronted with a difficult objective test, students often panic and do more poorly than they might have had they used a disciplined approach to the exam. An effective strategy is to divide the testing experience into four main phases:

1 Get credit for what you know; answer only the items that you feel you can answer correctly.

In this phase, you read a test item, answer it if you are fairly sure of the correct answer, and skip it if you aren't. You want to answer the easy questions first to make sure that you get credit for what you know. If time runs out before you finish, you want to be working on items you have doubts about, not leave unfinished items toward the end of the test that you could have answered easily.

This phase also helps you get off on the right track and control test anxiety. One sure way to get nervous is to frustrate yourself over an item or two early in the exam, trying to bore into the recesses of your brain for a detail that momentarily eludes you. If an answer doesn't come to mind quickly, just skip the item. Sometimes the answer will pop up later, or another item later in the exam might give a clue to the correct answer. In many respects, this first strategy lets you conduct a final review and make mental associations that may well help you as you go on to the later phases.

2 Go back to items you skipped in the first phase and eliminate items that are likely incorrect.

In the second phase, your strategy is to eliminate choices that are definitely or likely incorrect. This simplifies your choice and improves your odds if you are eventually forced to guess on the item. Although you cannot always identify the correct answer, you may be able to eliminate one or two choices on multiple-choice or matching items that are almost certainly incorrect. In this phase, you can apply some of the suggestions about language and logic made earlier in the chapter. You can justifiably be suspicious of answers that do not grammatically link to the stem of the multiple-choice item or the term you are trying to match. You may be able to apply simple logic to eliminate other items. In many cases, you can improve your odds dramatically; in others, you may be able to arrive at the correct answer by process of elimination.

3 Restate or rephrase the question to get a different perspective on it.

In the third step, you go back to the items you still can't answer, and try to tinker with the phrasing to see what impact it has. If you find yourself baffled at which of three remaining answers on a multiple-choice item might be correct, you could take each and join it to the first part of the question and consider it as a true-false item. As you consider each choice by itself, you might be able to determine that one is "more true" than the others. For example, in an economics test, this strategy might result in an absolute statement such as "Rising prices invariably result in decreased demand for a product." You might try substituting words such as *usually, often,* or *seldom* for *invariably* to see whether a statement somewhere else on the continuum described earlier might be more accurate. Temporarily altering or rephrasing the item may help you get a different perspective on it; just make sure you make the mental shift back to the original when formulating your answer.

4 Make the most logical guess and move on.

Sooner or later, despite the success you may have had in the first three phases, you will probably get to several items that just defiantly remain a mystery. All that is left is to consider whatever clues might be available, make the best guess you can, and proceed to any remaining items. Though at this point you might think that one guess is as good as the next, a few remaining guess strategies are at your disposal. The final section of this chapter illustrates some alternatives to "mental coin flip" decisions.

> Look for your choices, pick the best one, then go with it.
>
> PAT RILEY

Tips for When You Have to Guess

TRUE-FALSE QUESTIONS

1 IF THE ITEM HAS ANY QUALIFYING WORD OR EXPRESSION, CHOOSE "TRUE."
As we noted early in the chapter, we can work from the assumption that few things in this world are absolute. Teachers often add qualifying expressions to statements to make them more "true" or less arguable, so be on the lookout for words like *usually, often, typically, most,* and so on.

2 IF YOUR TEACHER HAS SHOWN A DEFINITE TENDENCY ON PAST TESTS TO FAVOR EITHER "TRUE" OR "FALSE" STATEMENTS, CHOOSE THAT OPTION.

3 IF NO TENDENCY HAS BEEN APPARENT ON PAST TESTS, CHOOSE "TRUE."
Researchers tell us that on most tests, "true" items outnumber "false" ones. This tip tells you simply to go with the only odds remaining.

MULTIPLE-CHOICE ITEMS

1 IF ONLY ONE OF THE REMAINING CHOICES HAS A QUALIFYING TERM, SELECT THAT ITEM.
Or, conversely, if only one item has an absolute term in it, reject that one and choose one of the others.

2 IF ONE OF THE CHOICES IS SIGNIFICANTLY LONGER OR APPEARS MORE CAREFULLY WORDED, CHOOSE THAT ITEM.
Remember the concept of precision in verbal expression: greater precision almost always requires more language. Also remember that teachers may add qualifiers to make the choice less arguable. Human nature being what it is, a teacher is simply not likely to put as much effort into the decoys as into the correct answer. An item that stands out as significantly longer than another is likely to be the better choice.

3 IF THE CHOICES ARE A RANGE OF NUMBERS, CHOOSE ONE OF THE TWO THAT FALL IN THE MIDDLE OF THE RANGE.
When making out a multiple-choice test, teachers usually first fill in the correct answer and then consider the decoys. It is more common to go at least one number lower and one number higher in the remaining choices rather than putting the correct answer at the high or low extreme.

4 IF ONE OF THE CHOICES SOUNDS OVERLY TECHNICAL OR JARGONISTIC, DON'T SELECT IT.
As we noted earlier in the chapter, instructors sometimes invent a term and plug it in as a decoy. Don't be fooled into picking such a made-up term. The student who may have missed several classes or simply not prepared well for the exam may see a lot of terms that look unfamiliar, but if you spent time preparing, you should be highly suspicious of anything in a test item that looks or sounds completely new.

5 IF TWO OF THE CHOICES ECHO EACH OTHER IN THEIR PHRASING, CHOOSE ONE OR THE OTHER.
This tip reflects another tendency researchers have noted. When a teacher fills in the correct answer on a multiple-choice exam, the first decoy that comes to mind often has structure or phrasing that parallels or is very similar to that of the correct answer. For example, if the answer to a geography question is "Tropic of Capricorn," the first decoy that comes to mind is likely to be "Tropic of Cancer." If the correct answer to an anatomy test item is "sympathetic nervous system," the first decoy the teacher fills in might be "parasympathetic nervous system."

In Sum

Objective items aren't inherently easier than essay questions, but they do require a different approach. The strategies described in this chapter can help you improve your ability to analyze such items and earn higher test scores. The next chapter focuses on the other main testing format, the essay exam.

Chapter 8

*M*anifest plainness, embrace simplicity.

LAO-TZU (6TH CENTURY B.C.)

Acing

Getting Your Point Across

Essay Tests

Clearly and Forcefully

Well begun is half done.

ARISTOTLE 175

(C. 384–322 B.C.)

Oh Test, Where Is Thy Sting?

Essay test. Many students cringe at the mention of those two little words. Maybe they find any type of "academic" writing intimidating. They labor several evenings over a composition for an English class, perhaps weeks over a research paper. And when they open up the midsemester history exam they have just been handed and realize that they will have to answer twenty-five objective items *and three essay questions* all in an hour and a half, the circuit breaker in their brain trips. Turn out the lights—the party's over.

Most students believe essay tests are inherently more difficult than objective tests. For the typical student who is capable of at least basic writing proficiency, such is not necessarily the case. Not everything about objective exams works to the student's advantage. First, as we noted in Chapter 7, the validity of a particular item often turns on the interpretation of a single word. Answers are either right or wrong; there's no middle ground. You can know a fair amount about what a particular objective question covers, misjudge precisely what the question is asking, and get absolutely no points as a result. Also, objective tests are largely "teacher-focused" exams. They often test narrow, discrete details selected by the teacher, phrased in the words of the teacher, and judged absolutely as "correct" or "incorrect" by the teacher.

> *There are two ways of meeting difficulties. You alter the difficulties or you alter yourself to meet them.*
>
> PHYLLIS BOTTOME

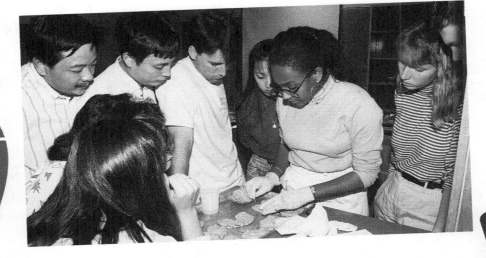

Essay exams, by contrast, are somewhat more "student focused." Sure, the teacher is still the one asking the questions. But in many cases, the student has some latitude in answering the question. There is seldom a precise or single "right" answer. Two students could write essays that have very different supporting details and both get full credit on the item. Most teachers try to measure the student's ability to make valid judgments about the focus of the question and then support those judgments with specific material from the course. A student can get at least partial credit for essays that are somewhat off the mark, as long as the answer uses a sound line of reasoning and offers fairly specific support.

Students often misunderstand teachers' expectations regarding the writing that is to be done on essay items. They assume that teachers grade essay items the same way they grade more formal compositions. The first step in taking the "sting" out of essay tests is to get a glimpse of what most teachers expect from your essay answers.

Expectation 1

Essay answers won't be polished compositions.

Instructors want and expect you to do the best writing you are capable of, but the constraints of the testing situation make what you produce much different from what you are expected to produce for an out-of-class writing assignment. Instructors will likely not expect you to devote time to a formal introduction and conclusion, unless you have a single *essayitem giganticus* and are able to devote a major portion of your testing time to its construction. You are expected to strive for clear, to-the-point writing. You can assume you're allowed to draw a single line through any mistakes and go on. (The testing situation rarely allows time for essay rewrites.) In most cases, content takes precedence over mechanics and style. This is not to say that a teacher won't mark and correct such errors; many teachers rightfully see their role as language coach for budding scholars. But such errors seldom factor significantly into your overall grade on the essay item.

In most cases, there is a variety of possible "correct" answers.

Students sometimes think that answering essay questions is an elaborate game of "Match My Answer." The teacher has in mind a "golden answer" for each essay item, and the students' job is to match it as closely as possible. Although a given instructor might ask essay questions on narrow, specific concepts with precise, "right" answers, many teachers quiz such concepts using objective items and reserve the essay questions for more open-ended inquiry. The true test of a student's usable knowledge is the

ability to narrow options, make decisions, and then discuss the concept intelligently. This is not to say that students have free reign—they still must answer the question they were asked. But most instructors allow students a fair amount of latitude, as long as they satisfy the burden of proof for whatever view they have taken.

To get full credit, students will have to demonstrate knowledge gained in the course.

An instructor might summarize this expectation by saying, "Show me what you have learned about this topic. State a belief, use valid support, and draw from *what you have learned in this course* to help you answer the question intelligently." Students sometimes complain that teachers say they want students to think and avoid regurgitating "right answers," but that students who do offer their opinions or show some originality are "rewarded" with poor grades. In such cases, students are often guilty of writing essays consisting largely of personal opinion or vague beliefs they might have held before taking the class. It is important to remember that students are typically expected to limit their support to the content served up in the course. Although opinions on a given issue may vary, both the student and teacher should draw from the same "data pool" when discussing that issue. Students should view the test item as an opportunity to confirm that learning has indeed taken place, and the only way to prove that to the teacher is to use information from that data pool.

Next, let's consider some general guidelines to help you perform better on essay exams.

Five Tips for Better Essays

1 DETERMINE WHETHER THE QUESTION IS PRESCRIPTIVE OR OPEN-ENDED.

First, examine the test item. Does it request specific information, or is it an open-ended question that allows you some degree of latitude? Prescriptive essay items typically are based in a specific "body" of information. They may refer to a specific concept in the text or perhaps elements from a lecture. Responses to such questions are more easily classified as "right" or "wrong." In the examples below, you can see that the instructor likely expects an answer that matches course material fairly closely:

Discuss the three main categories of nonverbal communication.

Identify and discuss the elements to be found in an effective lead sentence to a news story.

Describe the three elements of the psyche as outlined by Freud.

In each example prescriptive question, the phrasing suggests that a specific answer is expected. The use of the word *the* in the first example implies that describing two or four main categories is just not an option. In such cases, of course, you will first need to supply the anticipated main points and then go on to support or illustrate them.

Open-ended questions typically cover a larger scope and allow you some leeway in deciding just how to answer the item. Here are some examples:

What is meant by "nonverbal" communication?

What role does a "lead" play in a news story, and how is that role accomplished?

Discuss the most significant effects Freud had on the field of psychoanalysis.

Such questions allow for a variety of interpretations and answers. It is clear that the teacher does not have a "golden answer" in mind. Your responsibility is to state a proposition that fits the question and then provide main ideas and support to back up the proposition.

Neither category is inherently easier or harder than the other. Prescriptive questions are somewhat similar to objective test items: either you know the complete answer, or you don't. Open-ended questions require you to decide how to approach them. You may suffer from too many choices when it comes to determining just how you will answer open-ended items. Consider, for example, the task you would face with this far-too-general nightmare question: "Discuss World War II."

2 EXAMINE THE QUESTIONS TO DETERMINE WHETHER THEY CONTAIN "POINTER" WORDS.

If a teacher expects her students to take a particular approach to a question, she usually uses a word that points the student to a particular rhetorical strategy or structure. Listed below are some of the most common pointer words:

discuss Without any qualifiers, the word *discuss* implies an open-ended treatment of the topic; in phrasing like "discuss the four" or "discuss the main," however, the treatment is more narrowly defined. In either case, *discuss* implies more than just a superficial treatment of the topic: *Discuss the emergence of Romantic literature in England in the early nineteenth century.*

list The use of this term suggests that your answer need not be as detailed as an answer to a "discuss" question.

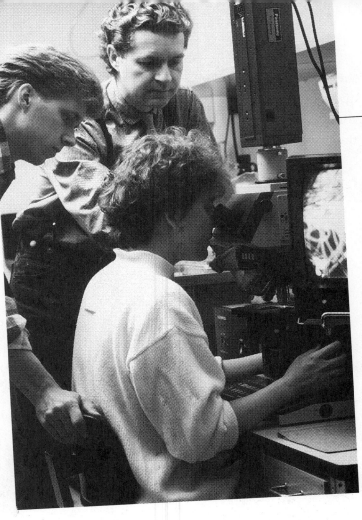

Focus on getting the list as complete as possible; if there are six characteristics of something, then you want to name all six, not pick and choose the most important, as you might with an open-ended "discuss" question: *List the characteristics that are typical of shock victims.*

describe This pointing word implies a focus on features and detail, perhaps physical detail: *Describe the features that distinguish impressionistic art from works of other artistic movements.*

analyze Analysis is the process of breaking something down into its component parts to determine what makes it "tick." When answering this type of question, you should focus on how the component parts work together to make up the whole. *Analyze* is often used in cause-and-effect topics: *Analyze the forces that combined to bring about the defeat of Nazi Germany in World War II.*

prove This term always points you to argumentative writing. You should present one side of an issue or idea, not both sides, and use a persuasive rather than informative tone. Supporting details need to be in the form of "evidence": *Prove that an object sitting still at the top of a hill possesses energy.*

trace This is one of the most popular pointing terms in history questions. It suggests that you should answer the question by examining distinct phases that occurred in a time sequence: *Trace the rise of fascism in Europe of the 1930s and 1940s.*

compare and *contrast* These pointing words direct you to consider the characteristics of two or more things. You usually do better to discuss each characteristic in turn (called a "point-by-point" organization of the essay), rather than all characteristics of the first item followed by all characteristics of the second. The word *compare* sometimes directs you to present both similarities and differences, though in a narrow sense, comparisons focus only on similarities: *Compare the use of exaggeration in two of Twain's short stories.* The word *contrast* always points you to an essay that deals with differences: *Contrast the Democratic and Republican presidential platforms in the 1992 election.*

Pointing terms can make the job of writing the essay easier, because they provide insight into the teacher's expectations about how a well-written item might be developed.

3 OUTLINE OR "MAP" YOUR RESPONSE BEFORE YOU BEGIN WRITING. Before you attempt to answer the question, always take a few minutes to make an informal outline or a concept map to determine what your main points will be and the order in which you will present them. Don't be reluctant to use up valuable test time to do this. A few moments planning your essay question can save you a great deal of time once you actually begin writing. Students who rush into answering an essay item often find themselves in the middle of it and suddenly at a loss to decide what to discuss next. They may get halfway through, not like where the essay is going, trash it, and then start over. Tinker with the ideas and main supporting details in the planning phase until you are satisfied with how they fit together; you should then be able to write without interruptions or digressions until you are finished.

As the next section of this chapter stresses, you want to make your essay structure obvious, and an outline or map helps you keep that structure clear as you write. Students writing under the stress of a testing situation can easily lose track of the question they are trying to answer and drift away from the topic, so an outline can serve as a valuable tool to keep the focus clear. Also, in a worst-case scenario, if the test period is concluding and you aren't finished with your last question, you can show your teacher the outline you are working from; he may be more

inclined to give you a few minutes to finish your work. Even if you are not allowed to finish, your teacher may give you a few points' credit based on the outline alone. A completely blank page won't get you a single point.

4 DON'T TAKE TIME TO WRITE AN INTRODUCTION OR CONCLUSION.

In a typical testing situation, you will probably have to answer two or three essay questions in perhaps thirty to forty-five minutes' time. If that's the case, don't waste your time developing introductory and concluding sections. State your proposition in the first sentence, and get on with developing it. When you have finished supporting your last main idea, quit. If the end sounds just too abrupt, write a short "clincher" sentence to wrap it up.

If, however, you have a major exam that is made up of only two or three questions that you have two or more hours to answer, you may wish to consider

treating each as a "composition" and develop brief but serviceable introductory and concluding paragraphs. You will still want to put 90 to 95 percent of your effort into developing and supporting your main ideas.

> Be careful
> that you write accurately
> rather than much.
>
> ERASMUS

5 MONITOR YOUR TIME.

Time has a tendency to race along when you are working on essay questions. Be sure you have a watch or clock at your disposal, and determine how much time you have to devote to each essay. Monitor the time, and discipline yourself to stick to the schedule you have set for yourself. Don't overdevelop the first essay and then rush feverishly to write skimpy paragraphs on the other two. And by all means, *use up all of the time you are allowed*.

Three Essential Elements for Eloquent Essays

You may encounter a wide variety of teachers, courses, and tests in your college experiences, but we can say with some degree of assurance that any well-written essay, regardless of type, has three elements. If you make a point of including these elements, you should be able to do well on whatever essay test you are served up.

Element 1

A clear, concise opening sentence that states the proposition you will develop

The first sentence is the most important sentence in the entire essay. It should serve two main purposes. First, its phrasing should clearly indicate which question you are answering. Some teachers let you choose several essay topics from a longer list. Even on exams where you don't have that option, there may be two questions on different facets of the same topic. You may also decide to answer the questions out of sequence, perhaps doing the toughest first. In any event, you want to make it crystal clear which question you are answering. Few things are more frustrating to a teacher grading a test than to read a student's essay and think, "Hmmm…interesting essay… Now if I only knew which question he was answering!!" You can be assured that every teacher who consistently gives essay exams has had that experience. You avoid the problem by making sure that your opening sentence echoes the phrasing of the question it is answering. (Do not, however, rewrite the question verbatim unless your teacher instructs you to do so.)

The first sentence should also state clearly and straightforwardly the proposition you intend to develop in the rest of the essay. Your essay is not just "about" a topic. You have an obligation to pose a proposition about that topic and develop support for that proposition. To put this idea into terms that you may be familiar with from composition classes, this first sentence is a thesis, or a central idea, for the entire essay.

If you can include in this sentence a reference to the main ideas that you will use to support the proposition, then by all means do so. Such a practice will help the teacher anticipate and interpret the ideas that follow.

It may help to think of this first sentence in these terms: if you *had* to answer the essay in a single sentence, this would be

that sentence. It would be a concise statement of what you know or believe about the question—the "answer in a nutshell."

Let's consider some examples of both good and bad first sentences of an essay responding to this: "Contrast two responses people often take to conflict: assertion and aggression."

> *Conflict affects most people on a day-to-day basis.* (Too general, and doesn't echo the question's phrasing.)

> *Assertion and aggression are two responses people often take to a conflict.* (Echoes the phrasing, but doesn't state a proposition.)

> *Assertion is one of the responses people take to conflict.* (Doesn't state a proposition, and sounds more like a statement of a main idea than "an answer in a nutshell.")

> *There are three main differences between aggression and assertion.* (A fairly good first sentence; it echoes the question, states a proposition, and identifies the number of main ideas to follow.)

> *Aggression and assertion differ significantly in terms of their objectives, their strategies, and their tones.* (An excellent first sentence—stating a clear proposition, echoing the question, and identifying its main ideas concisely.)

Element 2

A clear and obvious internal structure centered around two or more main ideas

This element accomplishes an important objective: it makes the essay item easy to grade. Imagine that you are a teacher for a moment. You have a set of twenty-five tests, all with three or four essay items. Like most teachers, your basic expectation is that students develop a proposition and support it with detail from the course. As you read each essay, you want to know what point the student is trying to make, what main ideas "prop up" the main point, and how detailed and valid the support is. Your main concern is not for subtlety or beautiful prose. You don't want to get lost in reading the essay, have to back-track, or struggle to see how it all fits together. Most importantly, you don't want the entire essay to be a "blob" of information that you have to sift through and try to make sense out of.

What the educational system tries to develop in the formal writing of most students is the ability to balance a concern for the importance of structure with the skill to communicate that structure subtly—to write clearly, but not to hit the reader over the head with the structure. The organizational pattern should not be so obvious and prominent that it calls attention to itself and becomes a distraction.

Being too obvious should *not* be a concern for you on an essay exam, however. Do whatever you can to make the arrangement of your main ideas readily apparent. Use obvious transitions between main points, start a new paragraph with each main point, or even underline each main point to draw attention to it.

Element 3

Adequate specific details offered in support of the main ideas

> A man's accomplishments in life are the cumulative effect of his attention to detail.
>
> John Foster Dulles

Ultimately, what makes or breaks the essay item is the level of support that is provided for the main ideas. It is one thing to state a proposition and to offer up some ideas as main points to support the proposition; it is something else to get down to the "nitty-gritty" world of specifics that support those ideas. Students often "talk about" their topic and main ideas, but the quality of their support goes no further than generalities or observations that almost anyone who had given a second thought to the topic could offer. Your primary responsibility is to draw from the course content and offer specific details, examples, "for instances," logical lines of reasoning to support the ideas—all concrete elements that provide a foundation for your entire argument. As explained in greater detail in Chapter 9 on academic communication, a good rule of thumb is that at least 50 percent of what you write should consist of such specifics. Providing reasonable support satisfies the burden of proof you have in any essay you write, and it should guarantee a respectable score on the essay, even when you have struggled with organization or the mechanics of writing. As we noted earlier, you want to take the opportunity to show your teacher that you have learned something in the course and can satisfy the obligation expected of anyone trying to show mastery in a subject area: *the ability to converse about the topic in specific terms.*

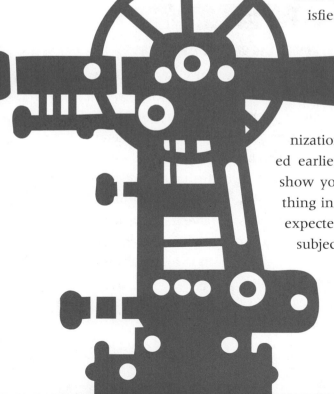

Reversing Roles: You Be the Teacher

Let's take all the theory offered up in this chapter and put it to good use. Let's imagine that you teach a course, perhaps a psychology or human relations course. You are grading the essay items written in response to the question used as an example earlier: *Contrast two responses people often take to conflict: assertion and aggression.* Below are the first six essays you have to grade. The item is worth 20 points. Consider the essays in light of the three essential elements described earlier. How many points would you give each? Grade them one at a time, putting the total number of points you would award in the blank provided. Then read the analysis. No peeking!

Essay I

Assertion and aggression are two responses people take to conflict. When a person uses assertion, he behaves assertively. In other words, instead of all the other options available, he asserts himself in his dealings with the other person. An assertive person behaves respectably in the conflict. He considers the situation, weighs the alternatives, and avoids the use of aggression. As we learned in class, aggression has some distinct disadvantages. It is also one of the most common types of responses that people make, once they decide to stop putting off a confrontation. The problem with aggression is that it can sometimes just blow up in your face. Aggression usually doesn't win you any friends, and it sure can make enemies. On the other hand, an assertive strategy can pay big dividends in the relationship, since it often results in much better decisions and strategies. Aggression usually doesn't result in too many effective decisions and strategies. Thus, the differences in assertion and aggression are both significant and profound.

POINT TOTAL FOR ESSAY I: _____

173

Analysis of Essay I: You don't have to be psychic to see that the writer of this essay knows very little specific information about the topic. The first sentence is only fair; it echoes the question but doesn't state much of a proposition. The essay is not clearly organized around any main ideas; the focus shifts back and forth between aggression and assertion but not according to any clear organizational plan. The observations are limited to very general "good/bad" judgments about assertion and aggression.

Essay II

Conflict is a problem that we all face at one time or another. As we learned in class, every relationship has some conflict—it's inevitable. The big issue is how people choose to respond to conflict. Sometimes they take avoidance strategies or just accommodate the other person as the path of least resistance. But once they decide to confront the conflict openly, they choose either an assertive or an aggressive approach. Assertiveness is a strategy that usually produces good outcomes to the conflict. Assertiveness means that you are simply trying to have your needs met, not trying to defeat the other person. Assertive people are basically just trying to be problem solvers. With a little luck, both people in a conflict can find ways to meet their needs without attacking or trying to defeat the other. Aggression is, unfortunately, a more common approach to conflicts. In worst-case situations, aggressive conflicts can lead to escalating emotions and physical conflicts. The strategy of the aggressor is to defeat the other guy no matter what. Sometimes the original issue gets lost somewhere along the way. Aggressive strategies have little chance of turning out well. Thus, assertion and aggression have some significant points of contrast. They are two of the ways people can respond to conflicts. Conflicts occur in all relationships, and people would be wise to learn to deal with their conflicts in productive ways.

POINT TOTAL FOR ESSAY II: _____

Analysis of Essay II: This is an improvement over the first essay, but it has its flaws. First, it has several sentences of an "introduction" and several more for concluding comments, neither of which is justified in an essay of this length. The very first sentence doesn't make it clear that the entire essay is about aggression and assertion, so a teacher grading this essay would start off with a question mark in his mind. No main ideas stand out clearly in the essay. The student also did not take to heart the pointing word *contrast* in the question, since the characteristics of the two topics aren't clearly stated and spelled out alongside each other. Support is occasionally specific, but overall not especially strong.

Essay III

When people take assertive approaches, they are problem solvers. In aggressive approaches, they are combatants. Each sees the other as a force to be defeated. In assertive approaches, logic rules, because people are able to be more levelheaded when they aren't competing against each other. In aggressive approaches, emotion usually rules. Finally, assertion is more of a long-term strategy, because it focuses on the needs behind the conflict. Aggression focuses on winning above all else, so it has short-term results and often leads to a whole cycle of win–lose situations.

POINT TOTAL FOR ESSAY III: _____

Analysis of Essay III: This essay offers only a "skeletal" treatment of the topic. It starts by offering detail about aggression, not by offering a proposition statement. If you study the essay carefully, you can find main ideas, but they are implied rather than obviously stated. (It discusses the roles of the parties, the nature of the strategies used, and the length of the outcome.) Detail is much too skimpy. This student obviously knows something about the topic, but he has offered very little in the way of proof: he has failed to "seize the opportunity" to show what he has learned.

Essay IV

There are some important differences between aggression and assertion. First of all, aggression forces people into the role of combatants. Each person regards the other as a force to be overcome. This view of the other person as "the enemy" results in predictable behavior. People don't communicate openly and honestly with those that they perceive as opponents. If anything, the opposite is true. Secondly, aggression almost always promotes emotionalism. When people get emotional, they use weapons that are counterproductive to dealing with the problem: anger, tears, abusive language, intimidation, and even acts of force or violence. Another characteristic of aggression is that it almost always results in more conflicts later on in the relationship. Aggressive conflicts will almost always result in win–lose or lose–lose situations. One of the two persons in the conflict may "win" because he is smarter, stronger, or more manipulative. On the surface, the problem is solved: "to the victor belong the spoils." But as we learned in class, conflicts are driven by unmet needs. The loser in the conflict still has unmet needs, so the probability that the relationships will continue to have friction is very high. Losers are motivated to try to turn the tables and promote more, sometimes even devious, conflicts further down the line. Assertion is a more productive approach. People play the roles of problem solvers, and they use logic rather than their emotions. Assertion, because it tries to satisfy unmet needs, has the capacity to put a conflict to rest and therefore has a much more long-lasting effect.

POINT TOTAL FOR ESSAY IV: _____

> *Analysis of Essay IV:* This essay starts off well, but it shows evidence of either poor planning or poor discipline during the writing process. The result is a "lopsided" treatment of the topic. Aggression is discussed in an organized fashion, with three main points. Each receives adequate support—the last one, probably more support than is necessary. The problem lies in the fact that the writer does not refer to assertion until near the end, devoting only three short sentences to it. Because the characteristics of assertion and aggression are not discussed "point-by-point," the essay lacks a sense of balance and does a poor job of contrasting the two approaches.

Essay V

Assertion and aggression differ in their focus, the roles of the participants, and the outcomes they usually produce. First, the focus of the two strategies is completely different. Assertive people focus on their own unmet needs. This is productive, because unmet needs are what created the conflict in the first place. For example, a couple assertively trying to resolve the issue of whether or not to have another child would try to determine what needs the child would satisfy in the partner who wants the child, and what needs would be threatened in the partner who is reluctant. The focus of aggression, however, is always on winning. The original cause of the conflict can often become secondary to win-

ning, because there is no motivation to examine the needs behind it. With the focus on winning, all the effort is aimed at bolstering your strengths and manipulating the other person into a state of weakness.

Another key difference is in the roles played in the two strategies. Assertive people are problem solvers. They are able to separate themselves from the problem and therefore can be much more logical about it. Problem solvers are also much more likely to look at the root causes of a conflict—the unmet needs. Because they view the problem as a mutual one, there is strong motivation for communication to be honest and straightforward. In contrast, aggressive people see each other as opponents. Opponents don't communicate well; if anything, they don't communicate at all or do so deceptively. For example, two people involved in a lawsuit are discouraged from contacting each other directly, because doing so might reveal information to the other side and weaken one's case. Opponents also are often very short-sighted: the only possible outcomes they see are "my way (right)" and "your way (wrong)."

Finally, the outcomes of the two strategies are almost always different. Assertive people, because they aren't locked into just two alternatives, can explore a variety of solutions. An assertive person sometimes sees that the best way to get what he wants is to help get what the other person wants, too—a win–win outcome. Needs aren't always "either–or." Sometimes both people can have their needs met, and the conflict is brought to an end. Aggressive outcomes are almost always win–lose or lose–lose. Labor negotiations, battles between nations, and marital conflicts can on the surface have "winners," but as history tells us, conflict goes on in the relationship and often erupts in other forms, because at least one of the two sides is left unsatisfied.

POINT TOTAL FOR ESSAY V: _____

Analysis of Essay V: (OK, so there wasn't much of a challenge in uncovering the diamond among the lumps of coal.) This essay does everything well. It starts with a clear proposition and previews the main points. Each main point is introduced in an obvious way, with transitions and new paragraphs for the second and third main points. Each main point is adequately supported with more specific detail, logical explanations of the main point, and "for instances" that demonstrate the student's learning. Each main point gets balanced treatment. Though only a bit longer than a couple of the other examples, it manages to present a detailed, well-structured treatment of the topic that is markedly better than its closest competitor. What's not to like?

Essay VI

Aggression and assertion are very different confrontation strategies in conflicts. One important difference is that assertive people use reason and logic as tools to solve the conflict, while aggressive people use force, intimidation, or gamesmanship. For example, my sister (Sandy) recently went through a bitter divorce, in which her husband (Robert) took on the role of aggressor. During the period of time before the matter was settled in court, he made a lot of threatening phone calls to her about how he had told his lawyer all kinds of things about my sister that would make her look like an unfit mother. He also tried all kinds of devious ploys to try to "win" their daughter to his side. He never showed her much attention while the family was intact, but just before the divorce was settled, he took her places and bought her gifts as a way to bribe her affection. He used every type of gamesmanship there was to win the battle. Also, like we learned in class, aggression usually doesn't result in many win–win situations. My sister's divorce destroyed everybody involved. Both my sister and her ex-husband spent thousands of dollars they couldn't afford on lawyers. (The lawyers were the *real* winners.) Their daughter seems pretty messed up, too. She learned quickly that she could play one against the other whenever she needed to, and you can tell that she isn't as happy as she used to be. Also, our parents and Robert's parents got to be good friends over the years, and now they don't get along very well either. Everybody turned out to be a loser in this mess. If Sandy and Robert had used an assertive approach rather than aggressive one, I'm sure the outcome would have been far less painful.

POINT TOTAL FOR ESSAY VI: _____

> ***Analysis of Essay VI:*** This essay begins well, but it demonstrates another fairly common flaw in student essays. It gets so wrapped up in illustrating a point that it "mutates" into a discussion of conflict in a divorce rather than a clear contrast of aggression and assertion. The first main point is stated as well as it could be in the second sentence of the essay. It is apparent that the student has learned a great deal in the course, because the application to the divorce situation is right on target. But the writer shows no discipline and no evidence of having planned the essay: although it starts well, the essay abandons its main purpose and continues to drift farther and farther away.

From these examples, you can begin to get a sense of the ideal "flow" of ideas in the typical essay you will be asked to write in the first year or so of your college life. The essay should begin with a clear statement of a proposition. It should then make an obvious statement of the first main point it will develop. Next, it should devote *at least* several sentences to presenting specific detail that justifies and "props up" the main point. Each subsequent main idea should be formally introduced and supported with similar depth of detail. Such a flow is a serviceable system for most every "entry level" college course, no matter what the discipline. With the foundation of this system in place, you will be well prepared to adapt to the longer, more demanding essay-intensive tests that you are likely to encounter in junior- and senior-level courses.

Chapter 9

Structuring Your Speaking and Writing

Understanding the Nature of Academic Communication

How forcible are right words.

JOB 6:25

Key Elements in Academic Communication

Every community has its own particular set of values. These values make life in the community much more predictable and harmonious, because its members have a fair idea of what is expected of them and what they must do to get along well with other members.

Perhaps you have never really thought of the academic world as a community, but it certainly is. Those most influential members of the academic community—the teachers—long ago adopted the community's values and carry certain expectations into each class, expectations that are not always clearly communicated to the students who themselves are trying to join the community.

One area where these values are quite consistent is in "academic communication." It may help to imagine academic communication in courtroom terms. Academic communicators—textbook authors, faculty members, and students— invariably find themselves trying to convince their audience of the validity of a particular idea, perspective, or point of view. Put another way, they have a "burden of proof" that they must meet. Whereas academic communication is often focused on the realm of abstract ideas or theories, the "evidence" presented to support these abstractions must be grounded in the world of specifics. Like a skilled prosecutor or defense lawyer, the academic communicator should make every attempt to tie details and conclusions together as clearly as possible, so the jury—the reader or listener—will be able to reach the inescapable conclusion that the burden of proof has been met.

Although the writing and speaking you do in the academic world may vary considerably in length, subject, and overall purpose, certain important elements remain constant from teacher to teacher and discipline to discipline. Understanding these elements and making sure you include them in your academic communication can go a long way toward providing for your success. This chapter offers a more detailed treatment of ideas expressed elsewhere in *Toolkit for College Success* about the communicating you will be expected to do as a college student. It presents a model for helping you understand how to structure your formal written and oral communication so that it conforms to the expectations of the academic community.

Five Key Elements

Whether you are planning an informal oral presentation, writing a ten-page research paper, or developing a response to an essay item on a test, most teachers will expect your work to have the following:

1 A singular purpose

Regardless of the work's length or complexity, most academic writers are expected to have a single overall purpose. That purpose may be as simple as introducing yourself to your classmates in a beginning speech class or as complex as evaluating the effectiveness of a president's administration in a lengthy research paper for your history class. In either case, you have one dominant purpose that motivates your work.

2 A clearly stated controlling idea

The purpose you intend to accomplish must be communicated to your audience in a clear, concise manner. In less involved works, such as essay exam answers, your controlling idea may be expressed in the first sentence. In more complex works, it is usually necessary to develop an introduction that leads up to the sentence that states your controlling idea. (Some teachers call this sentence a *thesis statement* or *central idea*.)

3 A clear internal structure marked by two or more main divisions

One element that many students overlook, but that readers and listeners most consistently expect in just about any work, is a division of the work into main ideas. One of the most compelling urges of the human brain is to look for structure in what it observes. The longer and more complex the work, the stronger the urge to group details into some meaningful organizational structure. Therefore, if you don't find a means to divide what you want to write or say into several main ideas, your reader or listener will struggle to do so. All but the shortest of works can easily become indigestible "blobs" of details unless they are arranged into main points. Your task is to divide or arrange the details into more "bite-sized" chunks of information. Doing so will help your audience see how the detail you provide relates to the overall purpose of your work.

How many main divisions should there be? Obviously, the term *division* indicates that there must be at least two main parts, and some works may logically divide into just two main parts. Typically, however, in all but the very briefest or very longest academic works, most writers aim for between three and five main parts. (One could argue that there is a nice symmetry to works that have three main divisions, but there is nothing magical about the number three.) It is usually not desirable to have more than five main divisions, because the reader or listener may find it difficult to recall what they were or how they related to each other. Keep in mind that the whole purpose of creating main divisions is to use structure to organize and streamline the information so that the audience does not have to work at understanding the relationship of the parts or at recalling what you said.

If you want to communicate with another thinking human being, get in touch with your own thoughts. Put them in order, give them a purpose, use them to persuade, to instruct, to discover, to seduce. The secret way to do this is to write them down, and then cut out the confusing parts.

WILLIAM SAFIRE

4 A sense of balance in the size of main divisions

Readers also expect a sense of balance in the treatment the author gives to each of the main points. If, for example, an English composition develops its first of three main points in about a page, the reader expects the other two main divisions to be presented in about the same length—certainly not a brief paragraph or several pages. One very short or very long main division that stands out from the others may lead the reader or listener to wonder whether he or she misunderstood a main point or missed it altogether.

5 "Weighty" supporting details

By far the greatest weakness most teachers see in their students' formal communications is a scarcity in supporting details for the work's main ideas. Main ideas are often stated and "talked about," but they are not always well *supported* by specifics: examples, detailed explanations, quotes, statistics, or other such elements. It might be helpful to think of supporting details in terms of the foundation on which your main points must be built. A good rule of thumb is that 50 percent of the written or spoken message should be made up of supporting details.

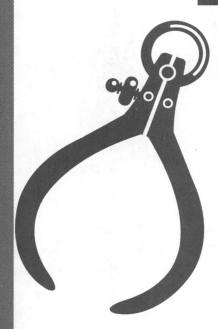

These five elements, therefore, underscore an important point: successful academic communicators must directly address both *ideas* and *detail* and link the two together in meaningful ways.

Let's consider an example of what happens when a student does a poor job of providing these five important elements. We'll assume that a history student has been asked to write a fairly brief in-class essay to illustrate his understanding of the differences between communism and fascism. Read the following sample essay carefully, and as you do so, try to be conscious of how easily you can establish the link between purpose, main ideas, and supporting detail.

What are some of the key differences between communism and fascism? This is an important question, since many people confuse the two or think that they are virtually the same. Men like Karl Marx and Vladimir Lenin were strong leaders of communism, while we often think of Mussolini and Hitler as the leaders of fascism. The two forms of government rose to prominence in Europe at about the same time, in the 1930s and 1940s. Of course, history shows that communism was much more long-lived than was fascism. Fascism was basically a movement supported by the wealthy industrialists and the military. Many people feel that fascism was a response to a fairly unique set of circumstances. Countries that were led by fascists had a weak history of any real democratic principles, and weak economies made the people in these countries frightened and open to the dominance of the strong-willed fascist leaders who promised them prosperity and power. Communism, on the other hand, developed as a social and economic movement with a definite philosophy behind it. The promises that communism held out to people made it popular with the working class, who were tired of the domination of the elite classes of society. The communist movement was very much a leftist or liberal movement. Fascist and communist countries were suspicious of each other, and each feared the other as well. The differences between the two were quite significant.

What is your overall reaction to that essay? Chances are you have a sense that the student "talked about" the topic, but could you summarize the main ideas right now? You would probably have to go back to the essay and figure out what main ideas it is trying to get across. The essay doesn't really have a clear controlling idea. Any differences between communism and fascism were left unstated; you would have to draw your own inferences to determine just what they are. Nor are there any main divisions: although the essay contains some valid details, they aren't clearly connected to anything, and in some cases they need to be more specific or explained further.

Now consider the following brief essay on the same topic:

Two fundamental differences distinguish fascist and communist political movements. First, communism had a clear philosophical basis, whereas fascism did not. The writings of Karl Marx, especially his *Communist Manifesto* and *Das Kapital*, laid out a social and economic basis for communism. Vladimir Lenin further shaped the philosophy. The writings of these men about the role of the working class and the necessity of its escape from the control of the elite classes attracted many educated people and free-thinking intellectuals. This philosophy laid out a groundwork and gave justification to the upheaval that occurred in Russia and other countries. Fascism, by contrast, had no real philosophy behind it; no one wrote any "fascist manifesto." Fascism was primarily a response of people to very weak economies and an unsettled political climate. Men like Hitler and Mussolini offered their citizens easy answers, stability, and a return to prominence and prosperity that their countries had once enjoyed.

A second major difference in the two political movements is that communism was primarily a liberal, or "leftist," form of government, whereas fascism was very conservative, or "rightist." Communism almost always emerged as a result of social unrest, in which the masses rose up to overthrow the ruling classes in such countries as Russia, China, and, later, Vietnam. However, fascism was most often a response from the middle and upper classes in an effort to maintain the status quo, not overthrow it. Mussolini and Hitler got at least the grudging support of the conservative upper and middle classes, along with the military, largely because the leaders offered the people protection from the type of unrest occurring in countries where communism was gaining a foothold.

Now apply the same basic test to the second essay: could you summarize its main points? Were the differences between the two forms of government clearly stated and explicitly laid out? The second essay, although only a little longer than the first, offers a much better response to the question. Its proposition is clearly stated, as are its main ideas. The emphasis in each paragraph is on support, with well over 50 percent of the writing given to examples, detailed explanations, or other forms of specific support. Every detail is tied directly to a main idea. The answer also exhibits a symmetrical arrangement of the ideas, with the two main parts receiving roughly equal treatment.

It is clear that academic communicators are expected to construct their messages carefully to ensure that a clear connection is established between several essential levels of information. There should be a "flow" from the statement of purpose to the main ideas that support that purpose, and finally to the details that support the main ideas.

Let's next consider a tool you can use to help you plan the formal writing and speaking you will be expected to do in your college classes. As you will see a little later in the chapter, this same tool can help you analyze the formal communications of others.

The Rhetorical Pyramid— A Planning and Analyzing Tool

The ancient Greeks introduced us to the term "rhetoric," which labels those collective skills in verbal communication that help us get our point across to others. The rhetorical pyramid depicted in **Figure 9.1** is a metaphor for the way effective communicators develop their ideas. As an organizing tool, it can help you plan a paper or oral presentation. Since it depends on a graphic metaphor that suggests that communicators basically "construct" their works piece by piece, the rhetorical pyramid is an effective alternative to the use of a topic or sentence outline. As an analyzing tool, the rhetorical pyramid can be used to evaluate the writing or formal oral communication of others.

FIGURE 9.1

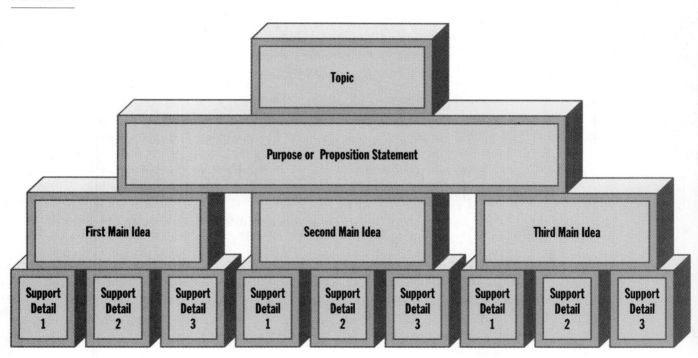

The image of the rhetorical pyramid as a structure presents a clear sense of the "levels" that exist within a rhetorical work—from the "higher," more abstract topic situated at the top, down to the concrete details used in support. The elements of the pyramid effectively divide the abstract from the concrete— distinctions that may be blurred in a conventional outline.

187

The metaphor of constructing a pyramid of ideas also reinforces the idea that supporting details are the foundation of any worthwhile rhetorical work. Main ideas and overall purpose can only be "built on" a sturdy foundation. You can see whether your work is balanced and sturdy by noting whether the required elements are present.

The Parts of a Rhetorical Pyramid

At the very top of the model is a small box **(Figure 9.2)** for listing the topic of the work. The topic is basically what the written work or presentation "is about." The topic might be a single word, such as "Recycling," or a phrase, such as "Global Warming" or "The Role of Nature in Stephen Crane's 'The Open Boat.'"

FIGURE 9.2

Topic

The second box **(Figure 9.3)** represents a purpose or proposition statement. Such a statement identifies the work's singular purpose or a perspective about the topic it will try to communicate. The statement should both clarify and limit where the work is going, as in the following examples:

"Recycling common materials is easier than you might think."

"Global warming poses a serious threat to the world's ecology."

"In Crane's story, nature is cast in the role of an uncaring observer of man's condition."

The purpose/perspective statement would appear in an identical or similar form in the introduction to the completed work, so that the reader or listener will know what the work focuses on.

FIGURE 9.3

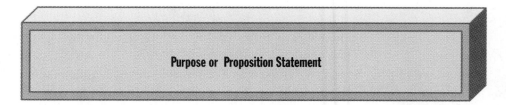

Purpose or Proposition Statement

The next three boxes **(Figure 9.4)** represent the work's main ideas, which, when supported by appropriate detail, justify or explain the statement of purpose. (As we noted earlier in this chapter, the actual number of main ideas typically varies between two and five.) For example, the three main ideas for a composition on global warming might be "increasingly severe drought cycles," "coastal flooding," and "threats to plant and animal life." Dividing the work into several main ideas helps the reader or listener "digest" the material more easily than presenting all the information in one single large section.

FIGURE 9.4

At the bottom of the model **(Figure 9.5)** are the boxes that represent the supporting details: the explanations, examples, quotes, statistics, or other specific elements that together justify or explain each main idea. The actual number may vary, but one single supporting detail will seldom justify a main idea. In the framework of the metaphor we are using, the supporting details must build a solid foundation on which the other parts of the work must rest. If the foundation is weak, then the entire construction will be unlikely to stand, as suggested in **Figure 9.6**.

FIGURE 9.5

FIGURE 9.6

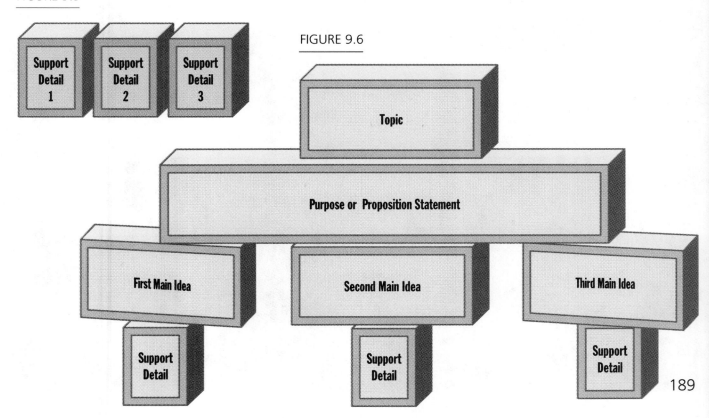

Other Uses for the Rhetorical Pyramid

Figure 9.7 is an example of how the rhetorical pyramid might be used to plan a speech on the benefits of recycling. As you can see, the pyramid can be used in much the same way as an outline, but "building" the speech in the following manner may help you see the relationships of the parts and ensure that all the components are present to create a "sturdy," well-developed speech.

As you can see, real world applications of a tool like the rhetorical pyramid won't always result in a perfectly symmetrical plan: the third main point has only two supporting details. Given the main idea, "recycling glass," however, the division into two supporting points as indicated is logical and adequate.

Rhetorical pyramids may be useful in other ways as well. You can use them to prepare for an essay test: take the topics you are most likely to be tested on, and construct rhetorical pyramids to clarify your perspective on each. If you do poorly on a written assignment or essay test, you might try to take the work and fill in a blank pyramid form to see what was lacking in your answer.

In addition to using this tool for planning, you can also apply it in analyzing or evaluating the written or oral work of others. If you are struggling to understand a difficult essay or article, you can try to use this tool to help you separate the main ideas from the supporting details. For example, read the following William Boot article, "The Clarence Thomas Hearings." The rhetorical pyramid in **Figure 9.8** on page 198 helps to clarify the supporting points for Boot's contention that the media did a poor job in its coverage of the Clarence Thomas–Anita Hill controversy.

FIGURE 9.7

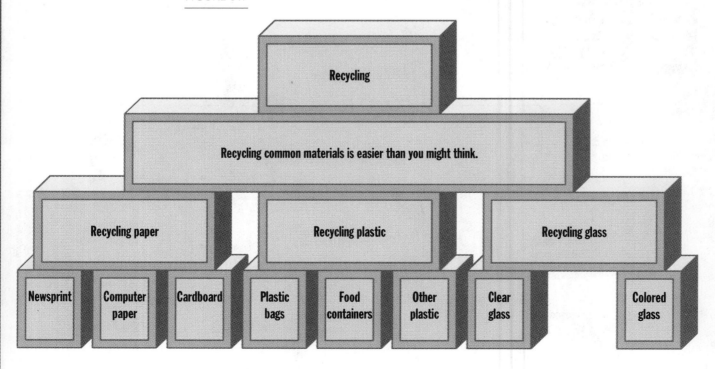

—

The Clarence Thomas Hearings

Why Everyone — Left, Right, and Center — Found the Press Guilty as Charged

WILLIAM BOOT

I T IS an old newsroom axiom that if reporting on a particular event draws protests from both right and left, the journalists on the story have probably done a balanced job. But what if the coverage prompts rebukes not only from the left and right, but from the center as well? What if it arouses the ire of countless generally apolitical people, black and white, female and male? What

William Boot is the pen name of Christopher Hanson, Washington correspondent for the *Seattle Post-Intelligencer*.

if it even provokes certain news organizations to attack each other's coverage? If all those factors apply, we can only be talking about the Clarence Thomas–Anita Hill sexual harassment dispute, which polarized the country and made for the most bizarre national news story to come our way in years.

Now that Thomas has been confirmed to the Supreme Court, it is time to take stock of the various objections to news coverage that this controversy provoked. First, an assessment of complaints from the right. Many conservatives were convinced that reporters were out to block Thomas by exploiting a news leak. Closely held Senate Judiciary Committee information had been disclosed to *Newsday's* Timothy Phelps and NPR's Nina Totenberg. Their stories about Hill's allegations jolted the country on Sunday, October 6 [1991]. Coming just two days before the Senate was scheduled to vote on Thomas, the leaks seemed to many to be politically motivated, timed to derail his nomination. The leaks prompted the Senate to delay Thomas's confirmation vote for one week, so the committee — under attack for not having taken Hill's allegation seriously — could probe the charges. For the first time Thomas's nomination seemed to be in real jeopardy.

Conservatives began denouncing the leaks with fierce indignation, demanding a formal investigation . . . and offering to pay a bounty of more than $30,000 to anyone who could identify the leaker. This reaction was, of course, part of a long tradition of selective outrage over leaks (a leak is monstrous if it hurts politically but not nearly so heinous if it helps, and Republicans themselves leak like crazy when it suits them). But what was the substance of their case against this particular leak? For one thing, they argued that reporting it was unethical, because it would damage Hill, who wanted to keep her allegations confidential. "This is going to be one of the saddest chapters in American journalism," Senator Alan Simpson predicted during an October 7 ABC *Nightline* confrontation with Totenberg. Casting himself as a protector of women, he said that disclosing Hill's name was like disclosing the name of a rape victim: "You've blown the cover of a person on a sexual harassment charge . . . you will have destroyed this woman." Of course, it was Simpson and his allies who immediately set about trying to destroy her. Judiciary Committee Republicans accused her of concocting her story and of committing perjury and eventually branded her mentally unstable.

There is no question that journalists trespassed on Hill's privacy in exploiting the leak.

Senate staffers had approached her, having heard that she had been harassed, and Hill had provided details on condition that they not be made public. But then someone leaked her affidavit to reporters, who leaped on the story. Thus, against her will, Hill was placed in the spotlight. On balance, this intrusion seems justified, considering that most of the senators preparing to vote on Thomas were not even aware of the allegations against him, and should have been. (Judiciary Committee members say they kept their knowledge of Hill's allegations under wraps to protect the privacy of the nominee and his accuser.)

Thomas's defenders also suggested that reporters who exploited the leak were, in effect, assassinating the federal judge's character on behalf of the Democrats. This argument confuses two issues — the motivation for the leak and the question of whether the allegations were true. The leakers may well have been Democrats out to get Thomas because he is a conservative (I'd be surprised to learn they were anything else). Even so, it is still possible that Thomas was guilty of sexual harassment. This surely was a serious matter that had to be explored by the media. Since the Judiciary Committee had opted not to explore it, reporting the leak was necessary to force the Senate into action. Reporters' responsibility is to try to get to the bottom of things, not cover them up, even if some news subjects suffer as a result. (It does seem that the possible motivations of leakers should be addressed in a story like this. What both the Phelps and Totenberg pieces lacked was a section that, without giving away the leakers' identities, could have suggested what might have prompted this disclosure at the time it occurred — i.e., only after Thomas's foes had exhausted their other anti-Thomas ammunition.)

Another, more considered, objection to the leak reporting comes from Brent Baker of the conservative Media Research Center. Baker argues that Phelps and Totenberg reported their leaks too hastily, recklessly jeopardizing Thomas's reputation before they had done enough reporting to justify their stories. He noted in an interview that Hill's allegation was far different from a claim that nominee X was guilty of something that definitely could be proven, such as stock fraud. Hill's allegation was an instance of her-word-against-his (as is generally the case in sexual harassment cases); there were no witnesses and real corroboration was impossible. Baker contends that, given those limitations and the inevitable damage to Thomas's reputation that disclosure would cause, Phelps and Totenberg should have held their stories until they had established, among other things, that there had been some *pattern* of misbehavior, with other women claiming he had been guilty of sexual misconduct with them. (*Charlotte Observer* editor Angela Wright eventually contacted the Judiciary Committee to allege that Thomas had put sexual pressure on her when she worked for him at the EEOC.)

Baker makes a strong case, but he does not give sufficient weight to the high-pressure situation in which Phelps and Totenberg found themselves. The Senate vote was just a couple of days away that Sunday, and if the story had not gotten out immediately there might never have been a Senate investigation. Given the time constraints, the two reports were not irresponsible. They cited "corroboration" from a friend of Hill's, who said Hill had complained of being sexually harassed at the time of the alleged conduct in the early '80s. The Totenberg piece carried Thomas's denial of the allegations. Phelps, unfortunately, could not reach him for comment, but he did include quotes from employee Phyllis Berry-Myers, who had worked for Thomas and who said it was inconceivable that he could be guilty of harassment.

Leaks aside, conservative groups like Baker's complain of a pervasive liberal bias in coverage. Even the *Wall Street Journal* editorial board got into the act, accusing *The Washington Post* and *The New York Times* of taking a "politically correct" pro-Hill approach to the issue (October 17 lead editorial). Conservative critics are able to cite some specific instances of slanted reporting (see

below), but overall it does not appear that liberal bias was much of a factor during the Hill-Thomas hearings. On the contrary: a report by the Center for Media and Public Affairs in Washington concluded that Thomas got much better press than Hill during the hearings. This study of some 220 network news broadcasts and newspaper articles found that, after the hearings began, nearly four out of five individuals quoted in news accounts backed Thomas. (Just prior to the hearings, a majority had been critical of him.) As to Hill, "more than three out of four [sources] expressed doubt or outright hostility towards her allegations." These data hardly suggest pervasive liberal bias. Instead, they suggest that pro-Thomas forces dominated the debate during the hearings on Hill's allegations of sexual harassment and that the media rather passively reflected this, just as they reflected the domination of pro-Hill advocates in the days prior to those hearings.

As to specifics of bias, consider these excerpts from the October 21 edition of *Time*, cited in the conservative newsletter *Media Watch*. *Time* associate editor Jill Smolowe wrote: "Given the detail and consistency of her testimony, it was almost inconceivable that Hill, rather than describing her own experiences, was fabricating the portrait of a sexual-harassment victim. . . ." In fact, it is not "almost inconceivable" that she was fabricating — the polls indicated that millions of Americans found the idea quite conceivable. In the same edition, senior editor Nancy Gibbs declared:

> *"Harriet Tubman and Sojourner Truth were slaves by birth, freedom fighters by temperament. Rosa Parks was a tired seamstress who shoved history forward by refusing to give up her seat on the bus. . . . The latest to claim her place in line is Anita Hill, a private, professional woman unwilling to relinquish her dignity without a fight."*

In fact, Hill is another Rosa Parks only if one assumes she is telling the truth.

Elsewhere, of course, one could find pro-Thomas biases. *The New Republic*'s Fred Barnes asserted without evidence on the October 12 *McLaughlin Group* broadcast that Hill was spinning "a monstrous lie," and Morton Kondracke, also of *TNR*, bolstered the theory, saying Hill might be compared to Tawana Brawley. John McLaughlin (himself no stranger to sex harassment allegations) compared Hill to Janet Cooke.*

For some less ideologically driven critics, a major complaint centered on sensationalism of this story. Political scientist Norman Ornstein, a barometer of centrist conventional wisdom, said in an interview that television coverage revealed warped news priorities at NBC, CBS, and ABC. They ran hours of Hill-Thomas testimony, whereas they had not provided live coverage of his pre-Hill confirmation hearings, at which big issues like abortion were on the table. This showed that ratings drove their news decisions and that personal scandal wins out every time over drier but equally important issues.

This is true, up to a point. Commercial networks do pander shamelessly. But as Ornstein acknowledged in a second interview, Hill-Thomas was, by almost any measure, a bigger story and deserved more coverage than the first round of Thomas hearings (where the nominee spent hours ducking the abortion issue and revealing as little about himself as possible). Once Hill's allegations became public, much more drama was to be had: there was a substantive issue (sexual harassment), and there were multiple conflicts (one man vs. one woman, men vs. women, black men vs. black women, women vs. Congress, Congress vs. the White House). And, of course, there was sex. Judiciary Committee chairman Joseph Biden described the high megatonnage of the story: "I know of no system of government where, when you add the kerosene of sex, the heated flame of race, and the incendiary nature of televi-

sion lights, you are not going to have an explosion" (quoted on an *ABC Town Meeting*, October 16).

Other objectors offered a kind of prude's critique, complaining that it was a travesty to bring all that graphic talk about Thomas's alleged references to sex with animals, and porn star Long Dong Silver, and pubic hairs on Coke cans into our living rooms, where children and old ladies could be watching. According to an ABC News poll released after the hearings, news media were rated lower for their Hill-Thomas performance than were the Democrats, the Republicans, Congress, or George Bush. One has to assume that the low rating was due in part to the graphic subject matter.

Of course, even those who voiced disgust kept watching. They could not do without the details. The story could not be told adequately without them. In fact, some TV journalists issued warnings to parents that simultaneously served as advertisements for the juicy material to come. Dan Rather, at the start of the Saturday October 12 hearings, said earnestly: "Now we want to *strongly* caution parents . . . there may once again be *extremely graphic testimony* that you may not want your children to watch. You may want to think about that." A few moments later, correspondent Bob Schieffer voiced awe at a case so unprecedented that it had forced the anchor of CBS News to say such a thing:

SCHIEFFER (*intense, portentous delivery*): *Let me just go back to the words you used at the start of this broadcast. We want to warn parents that what they may hear might be offensive to their children. Have you* ever *begun a broadcast of a Senate hearing with those kind of words?*
RATHER: *Never.*
SCHIEFFER: *It seems to me that this illustrates and underlines just how* very different *this is. . . .*

Come now, wasn't this laying it on a bit thick?

Enough of the prudes — on to the feminists, who had quite different objections. One was that the

---

*Cooke, a reporter for the *Washington Post*, won a Pulitzer Prize in 1981. After she won the prize and was questioned by her editors about her sources, she admitted the story was a "fabrication" and resigned.　—Ed.

news media, especially TV, were manipulated by the Republicans and used as tools to demolish Hill. Judith Lichtman of the Women's Legal Defense Fund argues, for example, that, during the hearings, journalists failed to draw the attention of viewers to Republican strategies and to the fumbling of committee Democrats. She contends that the networks and newspapers should have brought in experts to challenge questionable claims like the allegation that Hill had committed perjury, the insinuation that Hill might be "delusional," and Thomas's striking claim that he was the victim of "a high-tech lynching for uppity blacks." Instead, Lichtman says, most reporters were mere conduits: "The media portrayed what was presented to them — they therefore were manipulated. . . . We were let down by the media."

Lichtman is correct that reporters had seemingly little impact on public perceptions during the hearings. She is a bit off the mark as to why. Networks and newspapers actually did make some effort to provide the sort of commentary she says was lacking (as well as counter-opinion from conservatives). But, for reasons we'll get to shortly, this news analysis does not appear to have mattered much.

Here are some examples of the critical commentary. NBC's Robert Bazell, on the October 13 *Nightly News*, interviewed New York psychiatrist Robert Spitzer, who voiced extreme skepticism about the assertion that Hill was living in a fantasy world. Black commentator Bob Herbert on NBC's *Sunday Today* (October 13) sharply questioned Thomas's claim to be a victim of racism. In a series of live network interviews, sexual harassment experts like University of Michigan law professor Catharine MacKinnon disputed a Republican claim that no genuine harassment victim would have followed Thomas to a new job, as Hill did in 1983. (Hill went with Thomas from the Department of Education to the Equal Employment Opportunity Commission.) Reporters also tried to give audiences an idea of Republican strategy and

Democratic timidity. "One had the impression that . . . Orrin Hatch sort of played the part of Mike Tyson," Dan Rather told CBS viewers October 11. "Before Senator Biden could sort of get off his stool, Hatch was at him, all over him, and decked him." ABC's Tim O'Brien (*World News Sunday*, October 13) reported that Biden had acquiesced to Republicans, giving Thomas the big p.r. boost of live prime-time exposure.

As the opinion polls suggest, however, the impact of all this critical reporting was marginal. Why? The main reason, I suspect, is that this was a riveting live television event. Millions were watching and drawing their own conclusions. They did not need reporters to provide a news filter, so viewers may have listened even less closely than usual to commentary and analysis.

Live TV was only part of the press's "control" problem. In some cases, we lost control over some of our own debilitating impulses, which helped to undermine whatever small influence critical commentary might otherwise have had. For instance, there was the "Babble Factor": much of the intelligent news analysis (liberal, moderate, and conservative) was simply drowned out by the compulsive babbling and hyperbole that this event seemed to arouse in journalists. On October 11, Peter Jennings said of the Judiciary Committee, which has its share of dim bulbs: "One of the things we of course might remind people as they watch these proceedings . . . is that these senators are all profoundly intelligent men on this committee. In many cases they're all lawyers." Over on CBS, Dan Rather was groping for simple solutions. "If the FBI can't determine who's lying between the two, let's have some homicide detective out from Phoenix or New York City to spend a few days on this," he blurted on October 12. NBC's Brokaw said on October 11 that it would be bad if the hearings were to last several days because "it's in the national interest to have this all done as quickly and efficiently and completely as possible." As if doing it quickly were compatible with doing it efficiently and completely! (In order to meet the tight Senate-imposed timetable, the committee decided not to call any expert witnesses at all — making a thorough investigation virtually impossible.)

Then, for a few minutes on October 15, just before the Senate vote on Thomas, NBC seemed to lose complete control of its critical faculties. The network jumped from Capitol Hill coverage to Pinpoint, Georgia, where Thomas's mother could be seen live, rocking back and forth and praying in a neighbor's kitchen ("They're trying to keep him from helping us, Lord, but I ask you, Jesus, to please give it to him!" etc.). The sequence was captioned "NBC News Exclusive." The network seemed to be boasting, but why was difficult to fathom.

Another way in which journalists got sidetracked might be called the "Perry Mason Factor." Refusing to heed warnings from calmer heads, like ABC correspondent Hal Bruno, an astonishing number of journalists accepted a Republican comparison between the hearings and a trial. Republicans (and some Democrats, including the feckless Biden, at times) advanced the trial metaphor, emphasizing that Thomas must be judged by the standard of innocent until proven guilty, even though other nominees have been rejected on grounds of reasonable doubt and no candidate has a *right* to a seat on the Supreme Court. Reporters took the bait and reinforced a presumption-of-innocence message. "A political trial [is] effectively what we have going on here today. . . . There is a kind of trial aspect to all of this after all," said Brokaw during coverage of the October 11 hearings. "We have four institutions and people on trial . . . in a nonlegal proceeding," said Bryant Gumbel on the same broadcast. "I guess in a sense it is a trial in a way [and] we're seeing the defense lay out its strategy here," said Bob Schieffer over on CBS on October 12; "It is a trial in a way," agreed his boss, Dan Rather. And so on. By the eve of the confirmation vote, over half the public agreed that Thomas should get the benefit of the doubt, according to a CBS-*New*

York Times poll. Senate Republican leader Bob Dole said polls like that were what assured Thomas's confirmation.

Finally, there was the "Shovel Factor." Reporters (including me) failed to dig hard enough on their own during the Senate's consideration of Thomas. Why weren't the sexual harassment allegations against Thomas disclosed earlier? After all, Phelps of *Newsday* says reporters were hearing about the allegations as long ago as last July. Why wasn't more done to investigate Thomas's alleged taste for pornography, an allegation that became very pertinent in sizing up Hill's veracity? Why didn't reporters explain why Angela Wright, who complained that Thomas had sexually pressured her, was never called as a witness?

Before Hill's accusations became public, why wasn't more done to explore allegations that Thomas had breached conflict of interest standards? In one case, he ruled in favor of Ralston Purina, rather than recusing himself, even though his mentor and patron, Senator John Danforth, had a big interest in the company. In another case, Thomas was accused of delaying release of one of his controversial appeals court decisions, possibly to bolster his confirmation prospects. (Thomas denies any delay.) I was able to find fewer than ten stories devoted to the Ralston Purina issue and only a few focusing on the delayed ruling controversy. Meanwhile, as the left-leaning Fairness and Accuracy in Reporting group points out, news organizations ran dozens of articles about Thomas's climb from rags to riches — the Horatio Alger theme that the administration played up to divert attention from the nominee's meager judicial experience. Reporters had, once again, bought the Republican sales pitch.

Pro-Thomas salesmen continued to pitch successfully even after the nominee was confirmed, with Justice Thomas actively participating (which is highly unusual conduct in that Supreme Court members have traditionally been media-shy). Thomas cooperated in the ultimate puff piece, a seven-page, November 11 *People* magazine cover article, "How We Survived," told in the first person by his wife, Virginia. In it, she asserts that Hill "was probably in love with my husband" and that her charges "were politically motivated." She makes a point of describing the importance of home prayer sessions to the family. In a photograph illustrating the article, the two pose on a sofa, reading a Bible together. . . . [And] if new derogatory stories about the judge are broken in the months ahead, I would not be too surprised if we hear even more about the Thomas family's devotional habits — stopping short, one can only hope, of another urgent TV prayer bulletin from Pinpoint, Georgia. ∎

The article's main point is that all observers to the controversy seemed to find fault in the media's handling of the hearings. Although a quick glance at **Figure 9.8** might suggest that the second and third main points are a little underdeveloped because each has only a single supporting point, the examples given in support of each are quite detailed and specific; one could not argue that those points receive superficial treatment. In the first three main points, Boot answers some of the criticism and suggests that the concerns of biased observers were largely invalid. However, in the fourth main point, Boot, as a fellow journalist, takes his colleagues to task over three valid criticisms. The rhetorical pyramid helps the students establish a clear relationship between the topic, the proposition, the main ideas, and the supporting detail.

On the pages that follow, **Templates 9.1** and **9.2** are blank pyramids. You can duplicate these as they are or adapt them to meet your needs. You may also list additional supporting details under the bottom row of boxes if you wish to plan your topic in greater detail.

FIGURE 9.8

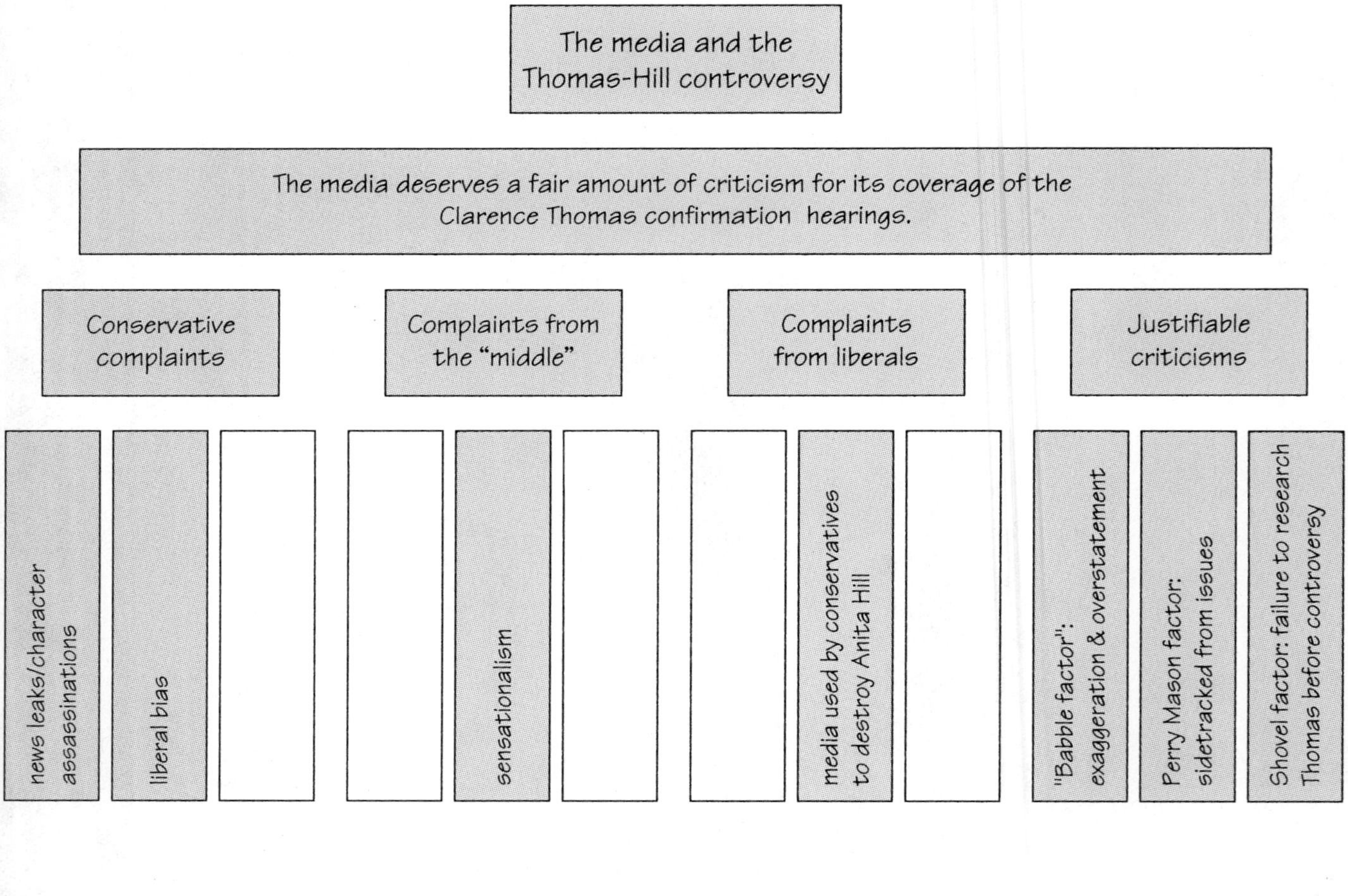

The media and the Thomas-Hill controversy

The media deserves a fair amount of criticism for its coverage of the Clarence Thomas confirmation hearings.

Conservative complaints | Complaints from the "middle" | Complaints from liberals | Justifiable criticisms

news leaks/character assassinations | liberal bias | | | sensationalism | | media used by conservatives to destroy Anita Hill | | "Babble factor": exaggeration & overstatement | Perry Mason factor: sidetracked from issues | Shovel factor: failure to research Thomas before controversy

Three-Part Rhetorical Pyramid

SEE OTHER SIDE FOR DIRECTIONS

Topic:

Proposition Statement:

Main Ideas:

Supporting Points:

Additional Details:

Directions for Template 9.1

Follow these directions if you are using the rhetorical pyramid as a *planning tool:*

1. Choose a word or phrase that describes what your work is about, and write it in the topic box at the top of the figure.

2. Determine what you want to say about the topic. What *singular purpose* do you have? Write this purpose or proposition statement as clearly and concisely as possible and put it in the second box from the top.

3. Next consider what *main ideas* you will need to develop to get your message across. Depending on the purpose you have established and type of communication you are developing, these might be major steps in a process, similarities or differences between two things, classes or categories of information, arguments for a point of view, or a variety of other major elements. Jot these ideas down as brief sentences or descriptive phrases in the boxes at the third level of the pyramid.

4. Finally, determine what *detail* will be needed to support each main idea and jot down descriptive words or phrases in the appropriate "foundation boxes" at the bottom of the figure. Be sure to list more than a single supporting detail for each main idea, and make these as specific and concrete as possible. Use the lines below the boxes if you need additional space or detail.

If you are using the rhetorical pyramid as a *text-analyzing tool,* follow these steps:

1. After reviewing the material, identify a word or phrase that labels the specific topic of the piece and write it in the box at the top of the figure.

2. Determine what you think is the author's main purpose for the piece. It may be stated quite precisely fairly early in the material and/or summarized at the end of the piece. Look at these sections for clues and write in the second box a summary of the purpose in your own words. If no direct statement of a purpose is apparent, consider the impact of the piece as a whole and summarize that overall message.

3. Consider the main arguments or points that develop the writer's purpose. Use headings and subheadings, transitional expressions, and paragraph breaks to help you determine what main ideas are being developed to justify your acceptance of the author's purpose. Write descriptive words or phrases for these main ideas in the boxes at the third level of the rhetorical pyramid.

4. Now look for supporting details. Write these down in the boxes below the main idea each is supporting. You can use the lines at the very bottom if you wish to list additional detail.

Four-Part Rhetorical Pyramid

SEE OTHER SIDE FOR DIRECTIONS

Topic:

Proposition Statement:

Main Ideas:

Supporting Points:

Additional Details:

Directions for Template 9.2

Follow these directions if you are using the rhetorical pyramid as a *planning tool:*

1. Choose a word or phrase that describes what your work is about, and write it in the topic box at the top of the figure.

2. Determine what you want to say about the topic. What *singular purpose* do you have? Write this purpose or proposition statement as clearly and concisely as possible and put it in the second box from the top.

3. Next consider what *main ideas* you will need to develop to get your message across. Depending on the purpose you have established and type of communication you are developing, these might be major steps in a process, similarities or differences between two things, classes or categories of information, arguments for a point of view, or a variety of other major elements. Jot these ideas down as brief sentences or descriptive phrases in the boxes at the third level of the pyramid.

4. Finally, determine what *detail* will be needed to support each main idea and jot down descriptive words or phrases in the appropriate "foundation boxes" at the bottom of the figure. Be sure to list more than a single supporting detail for each main idea, and make these as specific and concrete as possible. Use the lines below the boxes if you need additional space or detail.

If you are using the rhetorical pyramid as a *text-analyzing tool,* follow these steps:

1. After reviewing the material, identify a word or phrase that labels the specific topic of the piece and write it in the box at the top of the figure.

2. Determine what you think is the author's main purpose for the piece. It may be stated quite precisely fairly early in the material and/or summarized at the end of the piece. Look at these sections for clues and write in the second box a summary of the purpose in your own words. If no direct statement of a purpose is apparent, consider the impact of the piece as a whole and summarize that overall message.

3. Consider the main arguments or points that develop the writer's purpose. Use headings and subheadings, transitional expressions, and paragraph breaks to help you determine what main ideas are being developed to justify your acceptance of the author's purpose. Write descriptive words or phrases for these main ideas in the boxes at the third level of the rhetorical pyramid.

4. Now look for supporting details. Write these down in the boxes below the main idea each is supporting. You can use the lines at the very bottom if you wish to list additional detail.

Notes

Chapter 10

The art of writing is the art of applying the seat of the pants to the seat of the chair.

MARY HEATON VORSE (1874–1966)

A man may write at any time, if he set himself doggedly to it.

SAMUEL JOHNSON (1709–1784)

Working
Improving the Way

with Words

You Write and Edit

Rethinking the Writing Process

Most of us have marveled at how easy writing seems to be for some people. We are amazed at the Stephen Kings, Tom Clanceys, and John Grishams of the world. We can imagine them sitting at a typewriter or word processor, every day churning out dozens of pages of effortless prose that will soon be in print and on the best-sellers list. On a less grand scale, we imagine those fortunate few students who have mastered academic writing and breeze through their assignments. If we could watch one such student in action, the scene might be something like the following.

The Myth of Sally Goodwrite

Once upon a time, there was an A-student by the name of Sally Goodwrite. Sally had to write a one-thousand-word paper for her history class. She had spent the last two evenings in the library amassing pages of notes, which she had neatly arranged in a binder. She sat down at her desk and pulled out some sheets of clean, crisp notebook paper and her favorite gold-plated Cross pen. After staring for a few moments at the blank wall in front of her, she began to construct an outline for her paper. As the outline began to materialize on the page, Sally was pleased to see that all the subpoints were parallel and neatly indented. Soon, she had 1½ pages of a perfect outline. She started to reverse the order of a couple of subpoints, but then she realized that her first instincts had been right, as they almost always were.

Satisfied with her progress so far, she moved the outline to the left side of her desk and pulled out another sheet of notebook paper. She wrote her name and heading at the top, just as her teacher wanted it, and gave the paper a catchy title. She skipped a couple of spaces and began to write the introduction. Occasionally, she glanced to her left to make sure she was staying with her plan. Soon the first paragraph was done. "Perfect!" she thought.

Then the words really began to flow to the page. In her flawless penmanship, she translated thoughts from her outline to her paper. Once or twice she struggled momentarily with the phrasing of a sentence, but she quickly worked out the problem.

Twenty minutes passed, then forty. As she neared the conclusion, Sally had to stop and flex her fingers to relieve a slight case of writer's cramp. She quickly picked up her pen and gamely continued. Before long, the conclusion was done. She put a period at the end of the last sentence and then casually began to proofread for any inadvertent errors. There were none. Just to be on the safe side, she decided to count how many words she had written. To her satisfaction, there were exactly one thousand words. Finally, she slid the paper into a brightly colored binder. She went to bed and slept peacefully.

This slightly exaggerated myth reflects the beliefs that many students have about writing: Some people are just born writers. Writing comes easily to them. They seldom make mistakes or have to rewrite anything. These lucky people outline their thoughts clearly and write them fluently.

An extension of the myth is that the rest of the world is left to struggle in an almost hopeless effort to get words on the page. If such people could only learn to make a decent outline, only learn to spell, only master the laws of grammar, then they, too, might become good writers.

The method of writing used by Sally Goodwrite might be called the linear approach. It proceeds in a straight-line fashion: choose a topic; gather information; develop a plan or outline; and write the introduction, body paragraphs, and concluding paragraph. It is assumed that if the planning phase is done right, the writing will "happen" properly and major revisions should not be needed.

The linear approach to writing has been taught to generations of students. Some students use it and are comfortable with it. They are able to juggle ideas in their heads and construct workable outlines. They have a clear grasp of what they want to say and have no trouble writing the parts of the paper in the sequence described. If you are such a person, by all means continue to use the linear approach. As the saying goes, "If it ain't broke, don't fix it."

Some students, however, struggle to use the traditional linear approach. Despite the fact that they have chosen a topic and gathered information, they can't write an outline, because the ideas in their heads haven't formed clearly. They labor over the introduction for much the same reason. Their thinking is not linear, so they struggle to make their thought process fit the mold of "correct" writing as demonstrated by the Sally Goodwrites of the world.

> *A writer is somebody for whom writing is more difficult than it is for other people.*
>
> THOMAS MANN

The writing community has begun to encourage many students to employ an alternative method of writing. Often called the "process" approach, this method suggests that for some students, writing evolves through a very different method. But before we turn our attention to the specifics of this alternative writing process, let's consider some general tips that can help most writers, both the linear and the process writers.

Some Radical Ideas about Writing

1 STOP STRUGGLING WITH OUTLINES.

If you have always found the outline more difficult to produce than the paper, or write it after you finish the paper only to satisfy your teachers' requirements, try something else. You might try using the rhetorical pyramid (described in Chapter 9) as an alternative planning tool. You can also begin the planning process by just jotting down phrases or trying to produce a map or branching chart to help you think through your topic and begin to consider structure. As the next section of this chapter describes, you may forgo the formal planning process entirely and just write. Find out what works for you, and use it.

2 WRITE YOUR INTRODUCTORY PARAGRAPH LAST.

Many students labor over the introduction as long as they do over the rest of the paper. Writing the introduction first suggests that you know exactly where you are headed in the paper in advance. By the time you begin seriously to work on the body of your paper, you do need to have a fairly clear purpose in mind, but you may want to delay writing the introduction until after you are satisfied with the content and structure of your body paragraphs. You may be able to choose a more appropriate tone, opening strategy, or other introductory device when you know more specifically what lies ahead in the rest of the paper.

3 THROW AWAY YOUR PEN; USE A WORD PROCESSOR.

The world of writing took a quantum leap forward with the development of versatile and user-friendly word processing software. Word processors allow you to make mistakes and correct them in a matter of seconds. If you want to move a paragraph from the first page to the third, you can do so very easily. Want to zap a whole paragraph? No problem. Weak spellers and poor typists can use the spell-check features to catch and correct most such mistakes. If you have been overusing a particular word, your software may include an on-line thesaurus to help you find an appropriate synonym. If you have not already done so, make the transition from typewriters or handwritten final drafts to the world of computers and word processing. Even if you don't type, an hour or two of work with a keyboard, or better yet, with a typing tutorial program, will have you churning out text at a speed comparable to that of your handwriting.

College campuses typically have several computer labs open for student use, and you should determine where these computer resources are located. If you aren't familiar with a particular word processor, ask the staff at the computer center to help you get up and running. You'll be surprised how quickly you will learn basic functions of word processing and how much power it can bring to your writing.

4 LET YOUR TOPIC CHANGE AS YOU WRITE.

This radical-sounding tip is based on the assumption that you *will* write more than one draft of your paper. Most students discover an interesting phenomenon when they write. Their topic begins to shift or evolve as they go along. *As long as the purpose of the assignment is being met*, such a shift is entirely natural and may even be desirable. Many students begin with a topic that is too ambitious or too broad to develop fully in the type of paper they have been assigned. Maybe they didn't know it was too ambitious until they were well into their paper. The scope, tone, or even the central idea may change as the thinking and writing processes evolve. You simply need to be sure that your *final draft* satisfies the assignment, has a single, clear purpose, and that all the paragraphs contribute to that purpose.

5 REMEMBER THE 50 PERCENT RULE.

Generally speaking, good writing is made up of two categories of information: information that introduces or states "ideas," and information that offers specific support for those ideas. The introduction of a work sets up the reader to understand the main section of the paper, whereas the conclusion provides a wrap-up, summary, or final perspective to the main point presented. Each body paragraph develops a key point or main idea that justifies or explains the work's overall purpose. But a significant part of each body paragraph, usually at least 50 percent, needs to consist of *specific* support offered to justify the "idea" of the paragraph. Learn to make a distinction between *stating* a main point and *supporting* a main point. For further information on this suggestion, check out Chapter 9.

6 DON'T BE CONCERNED ABOUT MECHANICS OR SPELLING IN THE FIRST DRAFT OF YOUR PAPER.

As we will see in the next section of this chapter, it's better to delay your concern for mechanics, sentence structure, and spelling until the later phases of the writing project. Your initial focus should be on the discovery, organization, and development of ideas. The analysis of sentence structure, style, and mechanics is a very different sort of thinking process. Most people find it difficult to maintain the flow of ideas if they stop every few minutes to consult a dictionary or grammar handbook. Give yourself permission to forget about style and mechanics until you are satisfied with the ideas you have on the page.

Getting the Ideas and Words to Flow

We have coined the term "writer's block" to describe the affliction many students feel when they just can't seem to get started on a writing assignment. After three or four attempts at an outline and a couple of opening paragraphs are crumpled up and tossed toward the trash can, most such students can't help but wonder whether there isn't another way to get the job done. For these students, the linear process of writing has never really "felt right." If you have struggled with that method in the past, it can be a liberating idea to discover that an alternate strategy that might suit you better does exist.

An Alternative Approach to Writing

The "process approach," which is described in the steps below, is considerably different from the linear method most students have grown up with. Both methods, however, require the same two preconditions to make any efforts to write fruitful. First, you must have in mind at least a general purpose based on the assignment or writing task you have been given; for example, to examine the causes behind a significant historical event, write a research paper on an important work of literature, evaluate a work from a reading list and apply its message to some element of the course, and so on.

Second, you need to have gathered data on your topic. In some cases, this step might include reading or doing formal research in the library. At other times, you may write on more personal topics and simply have to inventory your own experiences or opinions. Whatever the circumstances, it is pointless to attempt writing if either the assignment is unclear or you don't have any information on which to base your ideas.

Assuming then that those two preconditions have been met, let's consider the "process approach." This alternative to the linear approach suggests that writing can be broken down into five key phases: discovery, clarification, development, shaping, and refinement.

1 Discovery

Many students have difficulty planning or outlining a paper because they simply are not yet clear on just what perspective they want to take on their topic. Perhaps the ideas exist in an abstract, formless mass inside their heads, or maybe the students have gathered so much data doing their research that they are overwhelmed by it and don't know where to begin.

We usually think of writing as a tool to record the end result of our thinking. In the discovery phase, you use writing at the beginning of the process, as a tool to *generate* thinking. The abstractions you are carrying around inside your head are often difficult to deal with. Writing can be a useful way to extract these ideas, getting them down on the page so you can confront them more directly.

> I write to discover what I think.
>
> DANIEL J. BOORSTIN

The discovery phase works this way: Put away all notes or other materials, check your watch, and simply write on your topic for a preset time, perhaps fifteen to thirty minutes. Begin immediately, and try to write nonstop. Don't worry about sentence structure, main ideas, introductions, or thesis statements. Just write. If a sentence isn't getting you anywhere, stop it and start another. Don't pay any attention to mechanics, spelling, or punctuation. Just write. If you get bogged down, keep writing. Repeat yourself if you have to, write about the fact that you *are* bogged down—just *keep writing*. Let your mind flow freely and write what you want to write.

The reasoning behind the discovery step is that if you have done enough research, reading, or self-analysis to be ready to write, then somewhere in your mind there is a main idea or a purpose struggling to get out. Writing is simply a tool to empty onto the page the jumble of thoughts you have on the topic. Once they are on the page, they can be searched through and sorted. The writing and thinking process in this first step will help you take the collection of thoughts in your head and convert them into a more specific and tangible form that you can work on and improve in the following steps.

> The idea is to get the pencil moving quickly...Once you've gotten some words looking back at you, you can take two or three—or throw them away and look for others.
>
> Bernard Malamud

2 Clarification

With the first step accomplished, you should have at least a page or so of writing to work with. In the clarification step, the process approach continues by getting you to search what you have produced and try to uncover several things. The first of these is a controlling idea. With the restrictions of the assignment in the back of your mind, look through the material before you in an effort to identify one dominant idea. (Peter Elbow, in his *Writing Without Teachers*, suggests that you look to see what idea is "sticking its neck out.") When you find what looks like a statement that can serve as a controlling idea for your paper, underline it or use a highlighter to make it stand out on the page. Secondly, search for supporting ideas. These are the ideas or statements that directly support the main or controlling idea. Depending on the scope of your assignment, you may be able to find somewhere between two and four such supporting ideas. If you find such supporting ideas, underline or highlight them as well. Finally, search the information produced in the discovery phase to see whether any organizational pat-

tern has emerged. If it has, it will typically be reflected in the arrangement of the main ideas that you previously identified.

Let's consider an example. Your teacher has assigned a composition analyzing the theme of a short story your class has just read. In the discovery phase, you wrote about $1^1/2$ pages trying to explain your feelings about the story. Near the top of the second page of what you wrote, you uncover one sentence that fairly well states what you think the story is all about: "It seems like the author wants us to see that even 'good' people are capable of 'bad' behavior." You also see that much of the rest of what you wrote centers around several key episodes in the story, so you highlight the sentences that begin the description of these events, because they may represent the main points. No real pattern is apparent in what you have written, other than the fact that most of what you wrote is loosely arranged around the significant events of the story.

Take a clean sheet of paper (or go to the next page of your word processor), and jot down at the top the main idea you uncovered, along with any supporting points, arranging them in the most logical order you can. You are now ready for the third step.

3 Development

With the main idea and supporting points before you, begin to write your first draft of the paper. Your main objective in the development step is to state your controlling idea and supporting points clearly and begin to offer some detail to explain or justify the supporting points. Your writing is a little less forced and a little more thoughtful than it was in the discovery phase, but you do want to write fairly quickly and try to avoid getting bogged down. You may want to set a time objective for this phase as well, perhaps thirty to forty-five minutes. The finished product of this phase should be a longer version of what you wrote in the discovery step, with all of what you have produced related only to the key ideas you extracted in the clarification stage.

4 Shaping

Your attention now turns to shaping the work you have done into a well-developed, logically organized composition. You need to make some judgments about the three main parts of your paper and adjust what you have written to this point.

The Introduction   If you did not really develop a formal introduction to your paper in the preceding draft, do so now. The introduction should be relatively easy to write now that you have an initial draft of the body of your paper. You may wish to use a technique of some kind to start the paragraph—a quote, anecdote, rhetorical question, or other such device. In almost all types of writing, it is expected that the controlling idea for your paper be stated in a clear, concise form near the end of the introductory paragraph.

The Body Paragraphs   In most shorter works—compositions of three to five pages—you are typically expected to develop each main supporting point in a separate body paragraph. Check what you have written to see whether each body paragraph develops an idea that directly supports the controlling idea as stated in your introduction. Also, check to make sure that each body paragraph does more

than just *state* a supporting idea; it should offer specifics in the form of examples, explanations, quotes, statistics, or other such information to justify the acceptance of the paragraph's main point. Finally, note whether the body paragraphs go into roughly the same amount of detail. You may need to delete information from a bloated paragraph or add details to an underdeveloped one, but try to balance the relative size of the body paragraphs and give your paper a predictable symmetry.

The Conclusion   You probably have not yet written a conclusion as such, so you are ready to turn your attention to that task. Although the conclusion may be fairly brief, like any other paragraph, it does require development. In addition to providing a summary statement of your main idea, you may wish to use a "device," such as a final question or relevant quotation, to develop the conclusion.

Your primary objective in the shaping step is to complete a rough draft of your paper that is basically complete in terms of the *development of ideas*. If your draft consists of a series of detached paragraphs or major passages that have been "x-ed" out, you may want to rewrite the draft or edit your work using the word processor so that you have an identifiable "paper" ready for the final phase.

5 Refinement

Now that you are satisfied with the ideas your paper contains, you are finally ready to step out of the writer's role and take on the job of editor. The refinement phase focuses on making judgments about sentence structure, mechanics, style, and overall readability. A strategy for helping you proofread your paper is discussed in the next section of the chapter.

Proofreading a Paper

Many students doubt their abilities to proofread. To do the job well, they think, a person has to be an expert on grammar. Although a strong background in English grammar might come in handy, most students can do a decent job of proofreading their papers if they go about it the right way.

If you are a typical student, you are already a very sophisticated user of the English language. You have adopted many of the subtleties of the language and spent hours and hours writing it, speaking it, listening to it, and reading the words of others. Whereas you may not be able to *quote* rules of grammar, in many cases you are able to *use* those rules. When you encounter a sentence that has a problem, in many cases your "ear" for correct expression can help you improve the sentence, though you may not be able to explain to someone else the mechanics of what you did. The key is to follow a process that encour-

A powerful agent is the right word. Whenever we come upon one of these intensely right words in a book or newspaper, the resulting effect is physical as well as spiritual, and electrically prompt.

MARK TWAIN

ages you to focus on specific elements in your paper one by one. The steps below can help you do that.

Before you tackle the task of proofing your work for mechanical errors, try to find a classmate or friend to read your paper and react to what it says. Most people will gladly read your paper, as long as you make it clear you are not asking them to read in detail for undotted *i*'s and uncrossed *t*'s. Ask them to respond to the big questions regarding content. Does your paper have a clear controlling idea? Is the overall structure clear? Are any sections underdeveloped? Are any sentences confusing or especially awkward?

It helps a great deal to get another opinion about whether the ideas you have written about come across clearly. When *you* read the paper, everything may make perfect sense, but it is sometimes hard to separate the writing that actually exists on the page from the greater amount of knowledge you have in your head or the thoughts you stated in an earlier draft of the paper. Without this background experience on the topic, a peer reader should be able to indicate whether what you have written "works" or falls short. Take the comments of your peer reader under consideration, and make any revisions you think are justified before you continue to proofread.

One last reminder: *it is important to be satisfied with the content and structure of your paper before you go on to the editing or proofing stage.* Many students do not proofread well because they question and react to the *ideas* on the page rather than remaining focused on the task of *improving sentences.*

The process described below probably won't help you catch all the possible errors you might make in your writing; no single strategy can do that. But if you apply these steps to your completed rough draft, you should dramatically improve your ability to identify some common sentence problems and deal with them.

1 Visually isolate the sentences in your rough draft, and examine sentence structure.

Your objective in this step is to examine each individual sentence in a way that minimizes the distractions of the other sentences around it. There are two ways to go about this task. For the first, you will need two highlighting pens with contrasting-colored ink. Take the first pen and highlight the first sentence, stopping when you get to an end mark of punctuation: a period, question mark, or exclamation point. Then take the second pen and highlight the next sentence. Use the first pen to highlight the third sentence, and keep alternating colors until all sentences are highlighted.

In some situations, as on an essay test or an in-class writing assignment, you may not have time to give the sentences such a treatment. An alternate method that is almost as useful is to go to the end of your paper and read the sentences in reverse order. Read the last sentence first and evaluate as described below. Then read the second-to-last sentence and consider it. This strategy helps you mentally, if not visually, isolate the sentences by preventing you from getting distracted by the ideas on the page, since the ideas won't "flow" one into the other as they do when you read from the top down. Now consider the following as you examine the highlighted sentences.

If it sounds like writing, I rewrite it.

ELMORE LEONARD

- **Look for sentences that stand out as being much longer than the others.**
  These are not necessarily bad sentences, but you should look at them carefully to see if they are cumbersome or confusing.

- **See whether all the sentences are about the same length.**
  You may wish to vary the length of sentences to avoid choppy or repetitive sentence patterns.

- **Now focus on each sentence individually to confirm that it is complete.**
  Sentence fragments are serious errors, and most students can identify them if they simply read each highlighted section aloud and listen to determine whether the sentence sounds "finished" or complete. Any sentences that leave the meaning "hanging" or require another sentence to complete their meaning should be revised.

- **Finally, determine whether any of the sentences are compound, consisting of two separate and *complete* statements.**
  The transition point between these two parts should be obvious when the sentence is read aloud. There are only two "legal" ways to join complete thoughts in compound sentences: (1) by using a coordinating conjunction (*and, but, or, nor, for, so, yet*) and a comma; and (2) by using a semicolon (sometimes with a transition word such as *however, therefore, or thus*). Check to see that the compound sentences are joined in one of these two ways.

2 Justify every mark of internal punctuation.

Use a red pen and circle every internal mark of punctuation. Now examine each in turn to determine whether it is really needed. It is not possible to list every comma rule in this short guide, but you should keep in mind the following points:

The sole purpose of a comma is to mark a place in the sentence where a brief pause or a mental "shift" is needed for the sake of clarity. A comma NEVER serves as a connector, particularly between two complete thoughts in a compound sentence. (That function is served by the coordinating conjunction, as noted above.) To use a comma by itself to try to link two complete thoughts results in an error called a comma splice or run-on sentence.

Most commas are used in one of three ways:

- To mark a pause after a long introductory element in a sentence

- To mark a pause between two or more "equal" elements combined in a sentence

- To mark a pause around a sentence element that interrupts the flow of the sentence

Examine every comma you have used to see whether you can classify it into one of these three uses. If you can't, try reading the sentence aloud and determine whether a pause or a mental shift is *necessary* at that point to communicate the meaning clearly. If it is, leave the comma there. If the sentence can be read *naturally* without a comma to mark a pause or shift, then remove it.

Two other marks of punctuation are used fairly often, the semicolon (;) and the colon (:). The semicolon is most often used to link two complete statements when no coordinating conjunction is used; this sentence is such an example. The colon is frequently used to introduce a formal listing of some kind, as in the next sentence. "Three marks of punctuation were summarized in this section: the comma, the semicolon, and the colon."

3 Check for misspelled words.

A poor aptitude for spelling seems to be one of the cruel tricks nature plays on some of us. We don't really know why some people appear to have a gift for spelling and others—sometimes even the brightest among us—labor with it throughout our lives. However, we have to recognize that the academic and professional worlds still place a premium on accurate spelling. Misspellings are a distraction to most readers, an irritant similar to a snowy TV screen or scratches on a compact disk. They draw attention away from the ideas a writer is trying to get across. Some readers may even suspect that the writer's failure to find and correct these errors reflects a lack of concern for other elements of the writing process as well.

If you have already shown the good judgment to use a word processor that has a spell-check function, most of this task can be done for you electronically. Do not, however, feel that you can turn over 100 percent of the responsibility for accurate spelling to the computer. The spell-check will not identify errors of word choice or some typographical errors, such as *there* when *their* should be used, or *mad* instead of *made*.

What if you are not a computer user? Then the task of checking spelling is more tedious. The time-honored strategy is simply to go through your document, circling each word that you cannot be sure is spelled correctly and looking it up in the dictionary. The catch, of course, is that you have to have a fairly good idea of the spelling in order to *find* the word in the dictionary. But take heart, for there is one other alternative. For less than $50, you can buy a hand-held spell-checker. This calculator-sized instrument lets you type in the word the way it sounds to you, and then it will give you the word back, spelled correctly! For example, if you type in *privuhlij*, it will give you back *privilege*.

4 Read the entire draft aloud, and listen for other problems.

It is important that you read the paper *aloud*; reading it silently to yourself seldom has the same effect. In this last step of the proofreading process, you are depending on your ability to distinguish sentences that "work" from those that don't. Read the draft aloud and listen for the little voice that says, "That doesn't sound very clear ... maybe if I said it this way...." Depend on your ability to identify phrasing that is awkward, and replace it with phrasing that says what you want to say clearly. Whether you can explain to someone else just why a sentence needs fixing and how to fix it is not important. Use this last strategy to help you deal with repetitive word usage, awkward phrasing, weak sentences, or bulky, bloated writing.

The most valuable of all talents is that of never using two words when one will do.

THOMAS JEFFERSON

217

Chapter 11

Becoming

Getting Results from Research

a Skilled Researcher

Knowledge is of two kinds.
We know a subject ourselves,
or we know where we can
find information on it.

SAMUEL JOHNSON (1709—1784)

Libraries and the Electronic Age

There was a time when doing library research was viewed as a character-building exercise. A major research project was a rite of passage that most students dreaded and not all students survived (academically speaking). Libraries were formidable places. Research involved hours and hours of work. Students had to deal with the tedium of fingering their way through tightly packed drawers of card catalogs. Research in periodicals took place in six-inch-thick volumes such as *Reader's Guide to Periodical Literature* or *The Social Studies Index*. Once a student found a possible source, there was little more than a title to help her determine whether the source would be useful. As often as not, she would write down the call number of the book or publication information on the periodical, search the shelves to find it, and then discover that the book or article didn't really have anything of value for her topic. There were many blind alleys and dead-end streets. Hours of work would often leave the student with little to show for her efforts.

Libraries have made a quantum leap forward in the way they store and index their holdings, and there is little doubt that *you* are the fortunate recipient. If you want to find a character-building enterprise, you'll have to look elsewhere. In almost all college libraries, the card catalog has been replaced by an electronic one. Once you become familiar with its simple operation, research will take a fraction of the time it used to take. Research in periodicals is similarly streamlined. The volumes of *Readers' Guide* and other such indexes are beginning to collect dust, replaced by electronic indexes on CD-ROM discs and personal computers. Now you can type in a topic and in a matter of seconds identify a hundred possible sources. The same index can tell you whether your library subscribes to the periodical and give you a summary of a couple of hundred words to tell you what the article focuses on. Many such tools even print out all the publication information you will need to help you find it in your library. If you think of libraries of yesteryear as a maze with many dead-end streets, then today's modern library is a superhighway.

This chapter has three main purposes: (1) to help you understand the overall structure of the modern college library and the processes that you can follow to find information as quickly and easily as possible; (2) to teach you an orderly system of recording that information so that you can put it in an easy-to-use form to help you complete your project; and (3) to clarify some significant issues regarding the mechanics and ethics of using your research notes in the papers you write.

The Structure of the College Library

Although college and university libraries vary considerably in size and architecture, all of them feature three main sections: the "stacks," the reference section, and the periodical section.

The Stacks

The section known as the stacks dominates the library. This section consists of all bound works other than those in the reference section—typically, thousands of volumes occupying at least several floors in most libraries. The stacks are said to be "open" if students are free to find and check out the books on their own. Some valuable books or special collections are in closed stacks to which only library workers have access.

The Library of Congress system is the most commonly used system of cataloging works in college libraries. Works on similar subjects are grouped together on the shelf, and every bound volume housed in either the stacks or the reference section is given a distinct call number. Here is typical example:

TL
820
K33
1989

T is the letter for the main category, technology; L is the subject subcategory. All books categorized as TL deal with some form of transportation: auto, train, plane, even space travel. The number 820 further classifies the subject matter of the book. The designation K33 is a code classifying the author: K is the first letter of the author's last name, and 33 is a subcategory code. The date 1989 indicates the edition or publication date of the work.

The Library of Congress cataloging system is quite detailed and clearly defined. A specific work with a given call number at Gigantic State University should have an identical call number at Miniscule Technical College.

Listed in **Figure 11.1** are the main categories and some of the important subcategories used in the Library of Congress system.

FIGURE 11.1

A	General Works	PJ-PL	Oriental Language and Literature
B-BJ	Philosophy, Psychology	PN	General Literature
BL-BX	Religion	PQ	French, Italian, Spanish, and Portuguese Literature
C	History of Civilization		
D	General History	PR	English Literature
DA-DR	History of Europe	PS	American Literature
DS	History of Asia	PT	German, Dutch, and Scandinavian Literature
DT	History of Africa		
DU	History of Australia and Oceania	Q	General Science
E-F	History of North and South America	QA	Mathematics
		QB	Astronomy
G	Geography and Anthropology	QC	Physics
H-HA	General Social Sciences and Statistics	QD	Chemistry
		QE	Geology
HB-HJ	Economics	QH	Natural History and Biology
HM-HX	Sociology	QK	Botany
J	Political Science	QL	Zoology
K	Law	QM-QR	Anatomy, Physiology, and Bacteriology
L	Education		
M	Music	R	Medicine
N	Fine Arts	S	Agriculture
P	General Language and Literature	T	Technology and Engineering
PA	Classical Language and Literature	U-V	Military and Naval Science
PB-PH	Modern European Language	Z	Bibliography and Library Science

The Reference Section

In many ways, the reference section is like a library within a library. It uses the same Library of Congress system to categorize and index its works that the larger "stacks" section uses. The rationale for having a reference section set apart from the works in the stacks is partly a function of availability and partly of specialization. First, it is important to have a body of works in the library that are always available to users. Reference works in most libraries cannot be checked out. Therefore, you can depend on finding at least some information on just about any topic and not be concerned that the books you need have been checked out by others. The works in the reference section tend to be somewhat more specialized than those in the stacks, though this difference is a little more difficult to explain. The reference section has general reference works, such as encyclopedias, almanacs, dictionaries, and yearbooks. It also contains very specialized compilations: collections of famous quotations, brief biographical sketches, multivolume sets of literary criticism, bibliographies, handbooks on a variety of science and technology terms, and so on. Because of their specialized and concise nature, you would typically use only a page or two of information from a specific reference work.

The reference section is an excellent starting point for your research, particularly when your knowledge of your topic is limited. Sometimes an encyclopedia is a good place to begin your search. In addition to providing a concise description of your topic, many encyclopedias end each entry with a bibliography—an alphabetized list of the best-known sources of information on the topic. Many of these works can be found in the typical college library, so an encyclopedia bibliography is a quick way to identify the most widely accepted such works. Bibliographies are also often bound as a complete volume. Such works are especially valuable if you are doing literary research on a major author. A student doing a research paper on Steinbeck's *East of Eden*, for example, would probably find a book-length bibliography compiled by a Steinbeck scholar and listing hundreds of essays and books written about Steinbeck and his works. In a few minutes, that student could have a list of twenty or so articles that focus on *East of Eden*.

Another shortcut is worth noting. Because both the stacks and the reference section use the Library of Congress classification system, the same student could note the call number on the Steinbeck bibliography, walk to that call number section in the stacks, and in a few minutes' time be scanning through a dozen or more works of Steinbeck criticism. Next time you visit your campus library, spend a few minutes' time just browsing through the reference section. You will be amazed at the wide variety of useful works it contains.

As a result of the electronic age, the reference section in most libraries is shrinking in physical size but growing in usefulness. Many of the bulkier and costlier reference works are now available in CD-ROM format. The power of the computer to store hundreds of pages of data on a compact disk, as well as to sort and manage that data efficiently, is leading more and more libraries to purchase disks rather than books. In many libraries, you can find entire encyclopedias, the complete works of William Shakespeare, exhaustive dictionaries, and books of quotations on compact disks.

The Periodical Section

The third main section of the college library is known as the periodical section, so named because works in this section are published on a "periodic" basis: daily, weekly, monthly, quarterly, and so on. The periodical section holds works of general interest, such as daily newspapers and magazines, as well as highly technical newsletters and journals. Also considered part of the periodical section are the various indexes needed to help users find information on specific topics. As we noted in the opening of this chapter, such indexes include the old tried-and-true research tools such as *Reader's Guide to Periodical Literature*, *The Social Studies Index*, and *The Humanities Index*. There are modern computer indexes of general periodicals. Among the most widely used of these are Infotrac, Wilson Line, ABI/Inform, and Proquest. These computer indexes combine lightning speed with powerful search capabilities, and most are updated frequently enough to include magazine articles published only a couple of months ago. If you have not already familiarized yourself with the computerized index in your college's library, do so soon. It will make your life as a college student much easier.

Depending on the space and financial resources of your college library, a portion of the back issues of its periodical section are stored in some microform format. The term *microfilm* most often describes a long, narrow film contained on a spool. The film is loaded onto a special viewer, and the pages from the newspaper, magazine, or journal are projected onto a viewing screen. You can often print a photocopy of the page from the same machine. Periodicals stored on *microfiche* are somewhat easier to use and less bulky for the library to store. A typical microfiche card is about the size of a four-by-six-inch note card, and it can contain sixty to eighty pages of most magazines.

Now that you have an overview of the structure and contents of a typical college library, let's consider the next step: how to begin researching.

Getting Started: Three Questions to Ask Yourself About Your Topic

Getting started—sometimes that's the toughest part of the process. The difficulty most students face is that they don't know precisely how to begin because they have only a vague notion of what they are actually trying to find. You can get off to a more productive start if you ask yourself (and answer!) these three questions:

1 Is my topic "researchable"?

Students often begin their work with a topic that is too broad to research effectively. For example, a student who has decided to do a research paper on "the judicial system" and has done an electronic search on that topic would probably discover several hundred books in the library and a thousand or more magazine articles on his topic. If he were to narrow his topic to "the Supreme Court," the book list might number fifty or so, and the magazine index list drop to several hundred. If

he narrowed the topic further to focus on the landmark abortion case *Roe v. Wade*, he may find several books listed in the stacks, and perhaps a hundred or so in the magazine index. At this level, the topic has become researchable. He may wish to narrow it still further, since there is still no shortage of material available to him, and a narrower topic would give him a clearer focus and almost surely make it easier to write his paper. He could finally settle on the topic "*Roe v. Wade* and the 1992 presidential race." By doing a key word search (more on this later) in the electronic magazine index, the student might find a dozen or so articles that focus specifically on the abortion issue and its effect on the campaign.

Chances are fairly good that you will begin with a topic too broad in scope for the task at hand. Go to your library and try the "Goldilocks" approach. Do an electronic search on the topic you are considering. If you turn up more than a couple of dozen sources specific to your topic, then that's "too big." Narrow your topic, and do a second search. Find little or nothing? That's "too small." Continue expanding or shrinking your topic until you find a dozen or so works listed that appear to be specific to your topic. That's "just right!"

2 How much do I already know about my topic?

Another consideration is how much prior knowledge you bring to the task. If you know very little about your topic, you will find the research tough going. It will be difficult to gauge just from the titles of articles or chapters you find whether the information will be useful to you. Note taking will be difficult, because you won't know just where the research is heading. If your knowledge is limited, you should go through a preliminary step before beginning the "real" research. Depending on your topic, you might wish to begin in the general works section of the reference shelves. A brief encyclopedia article may help you get started. (Don't forget to see if the entry concludes with a bibliography!) If you are doing research on a literary topic, a variety of well-known works are available in the reference section to give you a quick overview of a writer's life, literary subjects, or major works. If you are researching a current events topic or social issue, use the magazine index to identify an article in a major news magazine that can give you some background on the topic. Look for feature articles at least several pages in length. Once you have acquired enough background knowledge on your topic, you are ready to make better decisions about how to proceed with the actual research.

3 Will I focus my research efforts in bound volumes, periodicals, or both?

Here's a "quick and dirty" guide to get you started:

- **If your topic is historical, literary, or "scholarly," start in the bound volumes.** It is probably best to make a quick check in the reference section to see whether there are any specialized bibliographies on your topic or author. As we noted earlier, such bibliographies are a real treasure, as another researcher has done a lot of work for you and identified the best sources available. If you find no bibliography in the reference section, use the electronic catalog to turn up something in the stacks. If you are working on a fairly narrow topic, you may not find a single book listed. *This does not mean that the library has nothing in its stacks on your topic!* What it does mean is that you need to consider what broader or larger topic yours fits into and do a search on *that* topic. For example, if our student searches *Roe v. Wade* and doesn't find a book listed, he should broaden his search to "Supreme Court cases" or "abortion" to find bound volumes likely to have information on *Roe v. Wade*. Once one such work is found, the student can turn to the index in the back of the book and look for references to *Roe v. Wade*. Chances are excellent that the book will discuss the case in several pages or more. The student can examine those pages, take notes, return the book to the shelf, and look for another book. By quickly checking index references, our student can examine quite a few books and find more than enough information to support his research. This process of finding books on broader topics and searching their indexes is a powerful researching technique when applied to bound works.

  If your search in the bound volumes turns out a dry run, you may need to continue in the scholarly journals or in specialized works contained in the reference section.

- **If your topic is a current event, social issue, high-tech, or general interest topic, start in the periodical section.** Although you might be able to find information in bound volumes on such topics, there are two disadvantages to starting the search process there. First, information in bound volumes is always "dated." By the time an author develops an idea for a book, sells the idea to a publisher, writes the book, and gets it to the publishing company for editing, printing, and distribution, a year or two have passed. By the time the book is marketed, reviewed, and purchased by the library, another year or two may have gone by. The current event is no longer current, the social issue has mutated, the high-tech topic is low-tech, and the general interest topic just isn't interesting any more. Bound volumes may still be useful, but you want to *focus* your work in the magazines, newspapers, and journals, which contain information that is at most a few months old.

  Another reason for starting your research in periodicals is that specific information is almost always easier to find there. The modern library has seen the happy marriage of the information age and the electronic age. Not only can we find almost any topic in periodicals, but we can also have computers do the "grunt work" researchers find most tedious. The computer will make an intelligent search through huge databases, come up with a list of articles (in chronological order, if we want), tell us which periodicals our library actually has, and then print the entire list out on a nice, crisp sheet of computer paper. What could be better?

227

Using an Electronic Index

Earlier sections of this chapter have referred to the power of electronic indexes, particularly their ability to perform "intelligent" searches of huge databases. Most modern libraries have some form of an electronic index, perhaps one index to function as an electronic card catalog for its bound volumes and one or more magazine or journal indexes. The technology exists to combine the two into a single database, and that is the direction most libraries will probably be taking in the next few years.

A computer is at the heart of each electronic database. In some cases, particularly with periodical databases, the system may be a stand-alone computer, probably with the database stored on a CD-ROM disk. The computerized index used to access the library's bound volumes is likely to be a much more powerful computer, with a dozen or more terminals linked to it. Each terminal is a station that the researcher can use to access the records in the database. It is also common to find these computers linked to printers that supply the researcher with a printed list of the information she has identified and wishes to use.

Some students may find themselves intimidated by the prospect of having to use a computer to do research. Perhaps they fear that they may do something to harm the system, or that they will get so hopelessly lost in the process that they won't be able to find their way out of the search. Neither of these issues need be a concern to you. The menu systems used by these indexes will prompt you almost every step of the way for information. You won't have access to elements in the program that could lead you to wipe out a record or do anything destructive at all to the index. If you should find yourself lost somewhere along the way and not know how to get back, the keyboard will have an escape key or key marked "start over," which will end the search and take you back to the opening menu. Such indexes typically have a "help" key, which will provide screens of information to help you use the index. The computing system will have adequate safeguards to protect itself and to help you navigate your way through the search process.

Libraries may use a variety of electronic indexes, but most handle searches in similar ways. Let's focus on how you can use the two main types of indexes, those for bound volumes and those for periodicals.

Indexes for Bound Volumes

The opening screen for most electronic card catalogs will list options for you to choose to begin your search. This opening menu will typically list at least three search options.

1. Title
2. Author
3. Subject

You would usually select a title search only if you already know the specific work you are looking for and want to see whether your library has it. (This might be the case if you were fortunate to find bibliographic entries in an encyclopedia article or an entire bibliography volume in the reference section.) In many cases, you don't have to list the entire title; you can give a "truncated," or shortened, title. For example, if you were searching to find the play titled *The Effect of Gamma Rays on Man-in-the-Moon Marigolds*, you need only type the first part of it,

such as "the effect of gam," to confirm that it is in your library's holdings. Most indexes will let you do a *title keyword* search, which lets you type in a word, such as *Gamma*, and get a listing of all the books in the library that have that word in their titles. This is a handy search when you can't remember an exact title.

An author search is helpful in determining what works your library has that were written by a specific author. Such a search would prove helpful if you were considering a particular author as the focus of a literary research paper. It might also be used if you found a particularly valuable work by an author and wanted to see if any related works by that same author were available.

Subject searches are probably the most functional in the typical researching situation. Subject searches are "about" a topic; they are inherently broader than the author or title searches. A subject search lets you find works when you have no author or title in mind, and most indexes let you enter two or more subjects to find more specialized works. For example, if you are trying to research the effect of the abortion issue on political campaigns, you could enter both "abortion" and "politics" to find any books that deal specifically with that issue. Such a search strategy narrows your focus and could save you hours of time searching through dozens of more general books on abortion and dozens of books on a variety of political topics hoping to find the occasional work that happened to deal with both topics.

Indexes for Periodicals

As we noted, periodicals are usually a much more fruitful source of information on current events, technical, or general interest topics, than are bound volumes. Electronic indexes for periodicals typically perform just subject searches, though the particular index will likely have a couple of options about just how those searches are to be performed. You can usually enter two or more topics to find specialized articles, just as described in the preceding section. For example, a recent search of an index called Infotrac illustrates just how useful such indexes can be. Let's say the researcher wanted some information on the controversy created by the abortion issue at the 1992 Republican National Convention. Typing in just the word *abortion* yielded 1440 magazine articles! When *abortion* and *Republican* were entered, the number of articles declined to 42. By adding the word *platform*, the search identified 8 articles. Thus, in only a minute or two, the researcher was able to turn up 8 articles devoted to the precise topic. To accomplish the same feat using bound indexes would probably have taken hours!

The benefits of electronic magazine indexes don't stop there. Many indexes put a marker beside the articles from periodicals that your library subscribes to, saving additional time that you might have spent trying to find an article your library doesn't have. Some indexes let you get a summary of the article with just another keystroke. You can quickly tell whether the article offers a detailed treatment and whether it has an informational purpose or perhaps more of a persuasive one. You can probably also mark on screen the articles you are most interested in and get a printout listing the title of each article, the magazine, the volume, the date, the page numbers, and so on. This printout not only helps you continue your search through shelves or microform holdings, but also probably supplies all the information you will need to record in your bibliography or "works cited" page.

Electronic indexes are the researcher's best friend. If you aren't already a convert and skilled user, drop by your library and explore the indexes it has. You'll be amazed at the power they bring to your work.

One final point about research: if your best efforts leave you questioning whether your library does in fact have the information you need for your project, seek out the help of a research professional. Most libraries employ a reference librarian who is an expert in how and where to look for certain kinds of information. Before you consider scrapping your project and starting over, drop by to see the reference librarian. Chances are good that he will be able to point you in the right direction so you can complete the process of getting adequate information on your topic.

Librarian's motto:
Know thy shelf.

Anonymous

Taking Research Notes

Here's a scenario describing the typical college student's experiences doing a research project:

Zack has decided to do the research paper required in his freshman composition course on the theme of guilt in one of Eugene O'Neill's plays. Finding the information is no problem for him. (Zack has taken to heart all the good advice in the preceding pages!) He starts the process by reading the play very carefully. He pulls out a fresh legal pad and begins to take notes on some important passages. A day or so later, he starts seeking out secondary source material from literary critics. He picks books by four critics and finds dozens of pages related to his topic. Zack jots down the bibliographic information in the margins of the legal pad. He fills several more pages in the legal pad from these works and checks out a few promising journal articles. These are excellent, too, so after taking notes on the articles, he checks over the work he has accumulated and finds he has more than fifteen pages of notes to work with. He feels confident that he has all the information he will need to write his paper.

The deadline for his assignment is drawing closer, so he begins to work on the first draft of his paper. He quickly becomes frustrated with the "blob" of information he has; it's difficult to find a particular passage or two that he knows he has somewhere, and he's spending a lot of his time turning back and forth in the pages. He tears out all of the note pages and spreads them out to make the process a little easier. In one crucial part of his paper, he quotes some excellent comments from a critic, but suddenly realizes he doesn't know *which* critic; there isn't any bibliographic information beside this quote. He mutters under his breath about having to go back to the library to try to find out which book it came from. A little later, he discovers that another piece of valuable commentary is lacking a page number. Still later, he questions whether a particular note

is a direct quote or whether he paraphrased the author's words. In the "eleventh hour" of his task, when he should be wrapping things up, Zack is making a mad dash across campus toward the library, hoping it will be open long enough for him to find out what he needs. "There's got to be a better way!" he thinks as he hurries through the aisles of the library.

Well, Zack is right—there is a better way. Finding the information you need is only part of the challenge of doing research. You need to record the information in a way that makes it as usable as possible. Follow this system to ensure that your note taking will be fruitful:

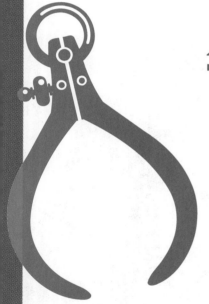

1 Use note cards rather than pages from a legal pad or notebook for your note taking.

Note cards are much easier to work with than pages of notes in a legal pad or spiral notebook. Note cards can be sorted and laid out in groupings by topic to help you measure where your support lies.

2 Create a bibliography card before taking any notes from a given source.

Once you find a source that you want to take notes from, begin by making out the bibliography card. The bibliography card will have all the information you will need when listing your sources in your paper's bibliography or "works cited" page. For most bound volumes, you need to record the author(s) or editor, the book's title, the publishing company, the publishing city, and the most recent printing or copyright date. The official source for this information is the book's title page. The publication date is often given on the back of the title page. For periodicals, list the author of the article (if given), the title of the article, the periodical's title, the volume number, issue date, and inclusive page numbers of the article. Other sources, such as encyclopedias and newspapers, require a different format for their bibliographic entries. To make sure that you are getting all the information you will need, it is best to consult the style guide (MLA, APA, Turabian, and so on) that your teacher has specified.

Also on the bibliography card, assign a letter to each individual source: the first source you take notes from should be *A*, the next *B*, and so on.

3 Use a cross-referencing system to tie each note card to the source's bibliography card.

By using the cross-referencing system as illustrated in **Figure 11.2**, you will know the source of every card and only have to write down this information once. All the note cards you create out of the source recorded on the *A* bibliography card will also be labeled with the letter *A* and numbered sequentially. The very first card will be *A-1*, the second *A-2*, the third *A-3*, and so on, through the last note taken from that source. Notes you take from your second source will be *B-1*, *B-2*, *B-3*, and so on. Thus, each card will have its own unique code, a code you can "plug into" your outline, rhetorical pyramid, or whatever planning system you use to prepare for writing your report.

4 Record important reference information at the top of each note card.

Before you record the actual note, be sure to fill in three pieces of information at the top of the card: (1) the letter assigned to this source on the bibliography card

FIGURE 11.2

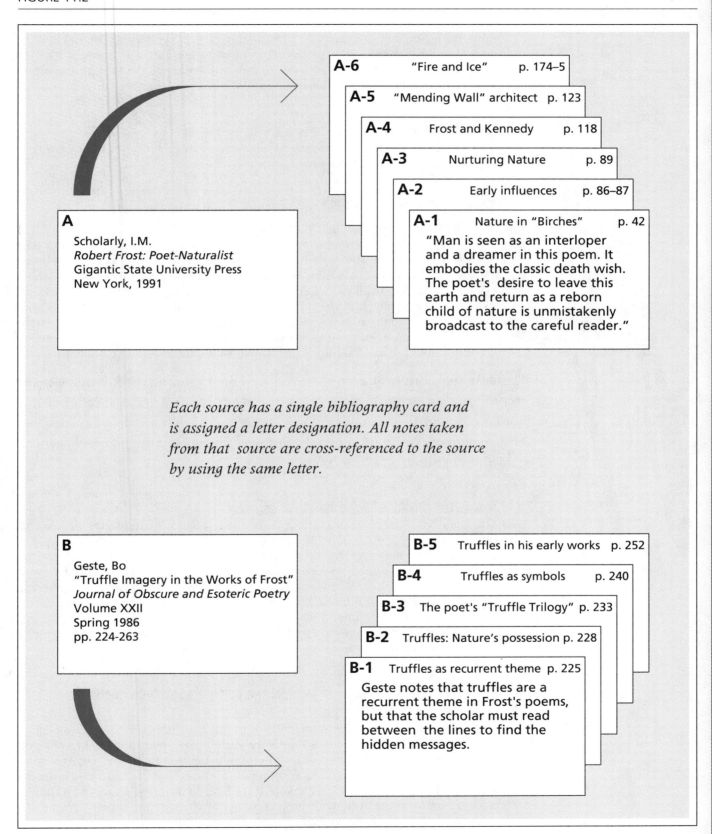

A-6   "Fire and Ice"   p. 174–5

A-5   "Mending Wall" architect   p. 123

A-4   Frost and Kennedy   p. 118

A-3   Nurturing Nature   p. 89

A-2   Early influences   p. 86–87

A-1   Nature in "Birches"   p. 42

"Man is seen as an interloper and a dreamer in this poem. It embodies the classic death wish. The poet's desire to leave this earth and return as a reborn child of nature is unmistakenly broadcast to the careful reader."

A

Scholarly, I.M.
Robert Frost: Poet-Naturalist
Gigantic State University Press
New York, 1991

Each source has a single bibliography card and is assigned a letter designation. All notes taken from that source are cross-referenced to the source by using the same letter.

B

Geste, Bo
"Truffle Imagery in the Works of Frost"
Journal of Obscure and Esoteric Poetry
Volume XXII
Spring 1986
pp. 224-263

B-5   Truffles in his early works p. 252

B-4   Truffles as symbols   p. 240

B-3   The poet's "Truffle Trilogy" p. 233

B-2   Truffles: Nature's possession p. 228

B-1   Truffles as recurrent theme p. 225

Geste notes that truffles are a recurrent theme in Frost's poems, but that the scholar must read between the lines to find the hidden messages.

and the sequential number of the note; (2) a brief phrase that describes the contents of the note; and (3) the page number or numbers the notes were taken from. The letter, by tying the note to a specific source, makes it clear where the note came from, and you will not have to write the publication information or even the author's name on the cards that actually contain the notes. The phrase at the top of the card provides a quick reference to the card's contents, and the all-important page number will be needed when you cite the work in your report.

5 Limit the focus of each note card to a single quote or idea.

Don't try to get too much information on a single card. Your notes will be easier to sort and classify if each has a singular focus.

6 Use a consistent system to identify quoted material from information paraphrased or summarized in your own words.

It's important that you be able to look at each card at a later date and know whether you have quoted or just paraphrased the author. The easiest way to make this distinction clear is to be careful to set off all exact quotes in quotation marks. The quotation marks tell the reader that these are the *exact* words of the author, and it is your responsibility to transcribe the information onto the note card accurately. You do not want to suggest that the author was a poor writer or speller by doing a poor job of transcribing her words. Take care to copy the quote precisely.

These six steps can help assure you that you are capturing the information and recording it properly on note cards, but many students face another crucial question: when to stop taking notes. There are no hard-and-fast rules about how many note cards are "enough," but you might keep the following general guidelines in mind:

1 Your notes should reflect a variety of sources.

You may have been lucky enough to uncover a book or magazine article that offers a thorough discussion of your topic, and perhaps you took a couple of dozen terrific notes from that one source. Count yourself lucky, but don't consider yourself done. A good researcher has the obligation to get the point of view of more than one author. You want to indicate that your paper or report reflects a balance of opinions and ideas. The number of sources necessary depends on the complexity of the assignment. Three or four might be a good number for a speech or composition, but a six- to eight-page research paper will probably require a minimum of a half dozen.

2 Don't stop your research until you feel you definitely have more notes than you can use in your project.

As you begin writing your first draft, you will find that some notes repeat or rephrase the same basic point. Some of the earlier notes you took might not be on topic, or your focus may have changed somewhat as you did more research. Most practiced researchers discover that they will use only one-half to two-thirds the total number of notes they have taken. It is better to have too many cards than to discover late in completing your project that you will have to "stretch" your existing notes and have only marginal support for your ideas.

On the Ethics of Research and Writing

No chapter on library research should overlook an offense that constitutes the most serious violation that can occur in the academic world: plagiarism. Plagiarism is the act of using another's words or original ideas and claiming them as your own. Plagiarism ranges from the blatant attempt of a student to pass off another person's work as his own, to the accidental misrepresentation of the authorship of a piece due to sloppy record keeping or careless writing.

The more blatant attempts at plagiarism occur when the writer knowingly affixes his name to work done by someone else. Such acts include copying an entire paper done by someone else or knowingly leaving out credit for quoted or paraphrased material from another writer. Depending on the severity and the assumed intent of such acts of plagiarism, punishment might range from dismissal from school to a grade of 0 on the work in question. In cases where the obvious attempt is to misrepresent the source of the information, the academic world's response is typically quite severe.

In formal report writing, students are expected to give the source for all quoted material and for all original "nonfactual" information that was provided in paraphrased form. "Factual" information is that biographical or historical data that could be confirmed in a variety of sources, such as an author's date of birth, educational background, family details, and so on. "Nonfactual" information enters into the realm of speculation or opinion that cannot be absolutely proved: that the author's birth was a burden to his family, that he hated school, that his wife divorced him because of his infidelity, and so on. Today, most such information is cited by putting the author's name and the page number of the information in parentheses immediately following the quote or paraphrased material, such as (Hemingway, 219). This "parenthetical reference" is typical to most style sheet guidelines, having replaced the use of footnotes.

Another more common circumstance of plagiarism on college campuses occupies more of a "gray area." Such cases include instances when a student doesn't paraphrase a passage properly and makes only superficial changes in language and sentence structure, *even when the source of the information is cited.* The experienced teacher can usually pick out such passages easily, because the sentence structure and vocabulary are often very different from what the student had been exhibiting up to that point. The teacher is likely to make a signif-

> *Do the right thing.*
>
> SPIKE LEE

235

icant deduction in grade when he finds such passages. The student must be careful not to use the phrasing and sentence structure that is essentially that of the original writer. If the original writer makes the point in an eloquent, concise manner, then the student should quote the material verbatim. Once a student makes the decision to use information in a paraphrased form, she must be careful to express the idea in her own words, still crediting the thought to the original writer by using a parenthetical reference or other accepted method.

The best way to ensure that you are using proper paraphrasing technique is to read the passage several times until its meaning is clear, close the book, and then write to summarize the passage *in your own words*. When you have finished, compare what you have written with the original to be sure that *your* words captured the basic meaning of the original quote.

Perhaps an example will illustrate the difference between the proper and improper paraphrasing techniques described above. Consider for a moment this quote taken from a work of literary criticism by Edgar Allan Poe:

> "If any literary work is too long to be read at one sitting, we must be content to dispense with the immensely important effect derivable from unity of impression—for, if two sittings be required, the affairs of the world interfere, and every thing like totality is at once destroyed."

If a student were to paraphrase this passage as in the example below, in which only a few words have been changed and the basic sentence structure preserved, he would be sitting squarely in that "gray area" referred to earlier, even if he uses a parenthetical reference to attribute the information to Poe:

> Poe notes that if any literary work is too *lengthy* to be read at one sitting, we *would have to be* content to dispense with the *very* important effect *derived* from a unity of impression—for if two sittings *are* required, the affairs of *our* world *would* interfere, and *anything* like *a sense of* totality would be destroyed *at once*. (Poe, 540)

You can see fairly easily that only minor changes have been made to the original. There is no evidence that the idea has really been processed by the student's brain or even that the student fully understands what the passage is saying. Contrast this poorly paraphrased example with the following:

> Poe argues that all literary works must be brief enough to be read in a single sitting. Since every work is to have a unified effect, a reader who would have to stop reading a piece and come back to it later could not experience its full impact, because the unified "spell" of the piece would have been broken. (Poe, 540)

This last passage clearly differs from the original in phrasing and sentence structure, indicating that the student has understood and processed the author's idea.

Another consideration concerning the ethics of research and reporting concerns how much information, either quoted or paraphrased, can be used in a paper. Most teachers have seen research papers consisting of page after page of

an almost unbroken string of quotes or paraphrased material. Students often think that reports are *supposed* to be heavily sprinkled with such information—after all, what was the point of taking all those terrific notes if they can't use them? But you must never lose sight of the fact that a research paper or oral report is supposed to be *your* work. A significant majority of what you are to produce should be summary details, conclusions you have drawn, perspectives you have taken on the topic—expressed in your own words. The role of the notes you have taken is to serve as supporting detail—the spice, if you will—for the dish you are serving up.

In short, the academic world expects *you* to be the creator and craftsman of the message you are delivering. You have the right to use the words and thoughts of others in support of the ideas you are expressing, but you have an obligation to use that information accurately and to give fair credit to those who have studied and written before you.

Index

Photography Credits

Front Matter
Hilary Smith: p.iii
Blake Ratner: p.xvi Used by permission of Carleton College

Chapter 1
Hilary Smith: p.1
Jim Kamp: p.5 Used by permission of Illini Media Company

Chapter 2
Jim Kamp: p.12 Used by permission of Illini Media Company
Isago Isao Tanaka: p.13 Used by permission of College of San Mateo
Rochester Institute of Technology: p.15 Used by permission
Hilary Smith: pp.16, 21, 33
Steve Handwecker: p.22 Used by permission of Illini Media Company
Patrick Tower: pp.34, 35
Dick Schwarze: p.35 Used by permission of Eastern Michigan University

Chapter 3
Hilary Smith: p.44
Patrick Tower: p.45
Mark Cowan: p.49 Used by permission of Illini Media Company
Illini Media Company: p.71 Used by permission
Brigid Nagle, p.73 Used by permission of Illini Media Company

Chapter 4
Patrick Tower: pp.89 (top), 94, 95, 96,
Sean Reed: p.89 (bottom) Used by permission of Illini Media Company
Hilary Smith: p.90
Steve Handwecker: p.91 Used by permission of Illini Media Company

Chapter 5
Hilary Smith: pp.112, 114, 115, 120
Nora Hipolito: p.113 Used by permission of Illini Media Company
Patrick Tower: p.119
Dick Schwarze: p.123 Used by permission of Eastern Michigan University
Illini Media Company: p.125 Used by permission
Ruth Galvez: p.126 Used by permission of Illini Media Company

Chapter 6
Reed College: p.128 Used by permission
Hilary Smith: pp.129, 130-131, 132-133
Bowdoin College: p.137 Used by permission

Chapter 7
Hilary Smith: pp.148, 149, 151
Steve Nelleman: p.159 Used by permission of Illini Media Company
Sean Reed: p.160 Used by permission of Illini Media Company

Chapter 8
Patrick Tower: pp.162, 164, 165, 166
Hilary Smith: p.163
Nancy Bundt: p.168 Used by permission of Carleton College
Dick Schwarze: pp.171, 173 Used by permission of Eastern Michigan University

Chapter 9
Dick Schwarze: p.180 Used by permission of Eastern Michigan University
Steve Handwecker: p.181 Used by permission of Illini Media Company
Sean Reed: p.183 Used by permission of Illini Media Company
Patrick Tower: p.185

Chapter 10
Isago Isao Tanaka: pp.204, 205, 209, 211, 215, 216 Used by permission of College of San Mateo
Dan Bigelow: p.207 Used by permission of Carleton College

Chapter 11
Dick Schwarze: p.218 Used by permission of Eastern Michigan University
Sue Weisler: p.219 Used by permission of RIT Communications
Mark Cowan: p.223 Used by permission of Illini Media Company
Ruth Galvez: p.226 Used by permission of Illini Media Company
Illini Media Company: p.231 Used by permission
Bowdoin College: p.237 Used by permission

Notes

Notes

Notes